The WANTED
OUR STORY, OUR WAY

WTTW

BⓍXTREE

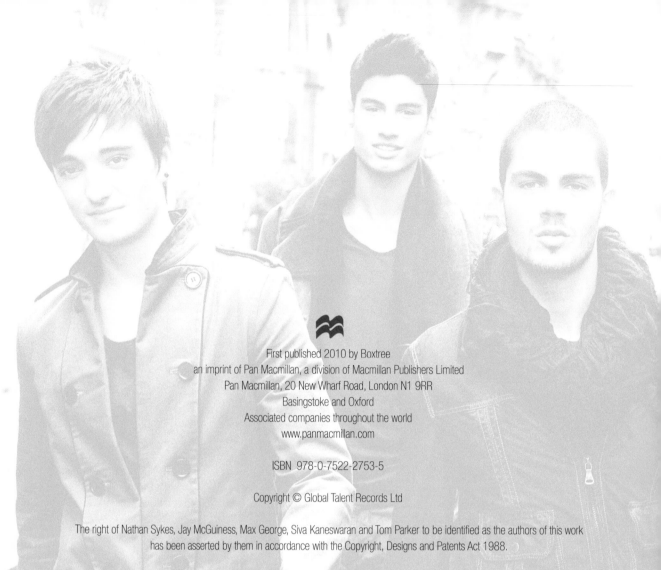

First published 2010 by Boxtree
an imprint of Pan Macmillan, a division of Macmillan Publishers Limited
Pan Macmillan, 20 New Wharf Road, London N1 9RR
Basingstoke and Oxford
Associated companies throughout the world
www.panmacmillan.com

ISBN 978-0-7522-2753-5

1 3 5 7 9 8 6 4 2

A CIP catalogue record for this book is available from the British Library.

Designed by seagulls.net

Colour reproduction by Aylesbury Studios Bromley Ltd

Printed and bound by Butler Tanner & Dennis Ltd, Frome

Visit www.panmacmillan.com to read more about all our books and to buy them. You will also find features, author interviews
and news of any author events, and you can sign up for e-newsletters so that you're always first to hear about our new releases.

CONTENTS

INTRODUCTION

We've already had some of the most amazing times. We've played tiny school gigs and massive stadiums; we've been followed to most corners of the UK by loyal fans; we've had a number one single; we've released our first album; we've worked with some of the best people in the music industry (and partied with a few of them too!); we've done TV, radio and awards ceremonies; we've been exhilarated, tired, nervous, happy … you name it. The last year and more has been an explosion of emotion for all of us.

We have loved meeting all our fans in person and online. Without them we wouldn't be here and we will never forget that. We've already been through such a lot together. The fans know so much about us, but there's so much more we want to share. We've each got a tale to tell, about our lives before we joined The Wanted. And, of course, from the first moment we sang together it's been a completely insane and amazing rollercoaster ride that's swept us up in the trip of a lifetime. And it's only just beginning …

It's hard to believe that five lads from pretty ordinary backgrounds have been given this extraordinary opportunity. We are all very different people as you will see, but there are a few things we share in common: we are incredibly grateful for the chance that we've been given, make no mistake; we are constantly amazed by our awesome fans and how they support us every step of the way. We want to make The Wanted a band that nobody will forget.

So here we are. This is our story, from childhood to the top of the charts and beyond …

We are The Wanted.

singing with this
group of lads for the
first time just felt right

The WANTED

There was always music in our house. Mum was a music teacher and even as a little baby she took me into her lessons, so I've been listening to music for as long as I can remember. As most of you know, I'm the baby of the band, born on 18 April 1993. When I was up in my room I could always hear Mum's pupils playing away downstairs. Mum was particularly amazing at teaching jazz saxophone, so I picked up a liking for jazz very early on. That led me to being a huge fan of artists such as Michael Bublé, but there were always Take That albums on in our house too, Whitney, Ray Charles, Michael Jackson and, of course, Stevie Wonder!

My dad is a health and safety manager and does a little bit of singing too. My mum and dad separated when I was eight, and whenever I went round Dad's house he'd have his guitar out, playing away. It's the same with my younger sister, who's also very musical. All my uncles play instruments, and one of them's an amazing pianist. Music was the soundtrack to my childhood. Perhaps that's why I couldn't be without music now.

The WANTED

music was the soundtrack to my childhood, perhaps that's why I couldn't be without it now

I started playing piano very young, but I quit at Grade 3 when my little sister Jessica started catching up with me – I was devoed! I didn't really enjoy classical piano at that age, which led me to writing my own stuff and putting my own take on songs I loved, singing jazzy versions of pop songs for example.

I was brought up in Gloucester. Where we lived was cool, it wasn't a rough town and it wasn't a posh town, it was just 'normal', an everyday place to live. I went to Longlevens Infant School, which was OK, to be fair. One of my earliest memories is of falling over in the playground and properly bashing my face in. I'd literally wiped off half the side of my face and I remember the teacher picking stones out of my cheek for ages. I enjoyed primary school in the main. I learned a lot, made tons of friends and the sarcastic side of my character came out too!

My first ever performance was when I was only six, at a holiday camp site when I just grabbed the mic and got on stage. I loved it and sang 'Deeper Shade Of Blue' by Steps while wearing this awful yellow outfit. Apart from that it was great! From that moment on I was hooked.

Even back then I used to do loads of singing – I would love to have been better at football, don't get me wrong, but singing was my thing. Unfortunately, a lot of the lads in class used to hate it and I got a fair bit of stick to be honest. Some days were tough, some weren't. I'd say I've probably been through what most kids go through. Nearly everyone has some experience of bullying at some point in their lives.

Looking back, the bullying was pretty pathetic. Sometimes it was because they didn't like the music I listened to – take the first gig I went to, for example, which was S Club 7. Then, when I was ten, I entered a Saturday kids' TV competition called 'Karaoke Kriminals', singing a Britney Spears song. It might sound wimpy – and I'd much rather have been singing Boyz II Men, which was the first record I ever bought – but I still won, and I was proud of that. Part of the prize was to actually meet and kiss Britney Spears. The lads at school really took the mickey out of

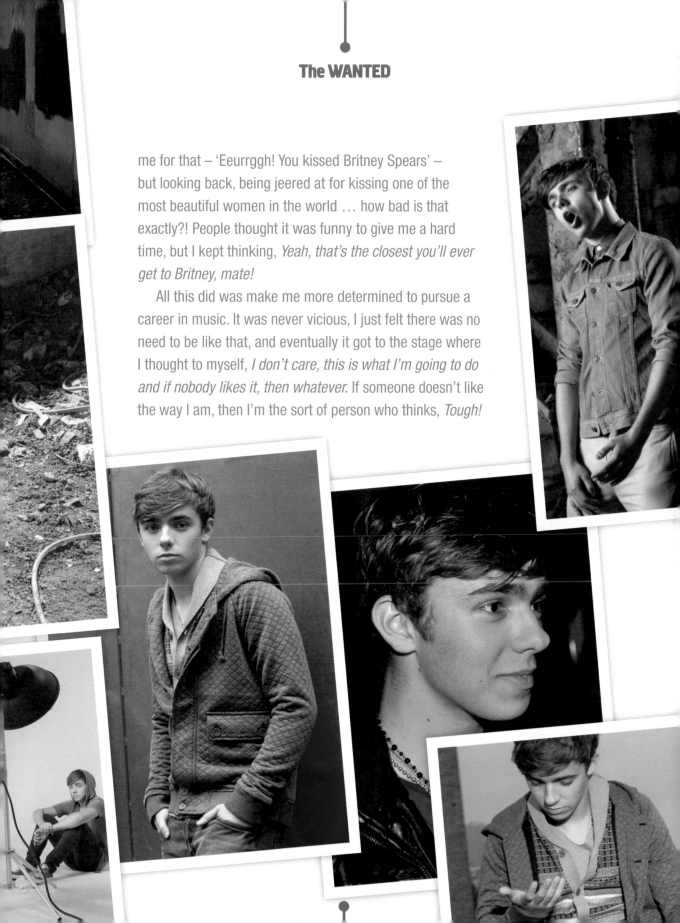

me for that – 'Eeurrggh! You kissed Britney Spears' – but looking back, being jeered at for kissing one of the most beautiful women in the world … how bad is that exactly?! People thought it was funny to give me a hard time, but I kept thinking, *Yeah, that's the closest you'll ever get to Britney, mate!*

All this did was make me more determined to pursue a career in music. It was never vicious, I just felt there was no need to be like that, and eventually it got to the stage where I thought to myself, *I don't care, this is what I'm going to do and if nobody likes it, then whatever.* If someone doesn't like the way I am, then I'm the sort of person who thinks, *Tough!*

my first ever
performance
was when I
was only six

By the time we came to the end-of-term fair, I just grabbed a mic and started singing, and I think people realized then that a) I could actually sing and b) I was really serious about it.

I was pretty naïve at that age, and apparently I was cute too. I entered loads of competitions, and the bigger the stage, the more I enjoyed it. For example, I've always loved football, it's one of my passions, and one of my dreams as a child was to perform at Old Trafford. When I was eleven, I entered a 'Talented Youngster of the Year' competition, and the final was at Man United's stadium. Looking back, my choice of song was quite brave, especially when you consider that I'd be singing it in a football stadium. I sang the Eva Cassidy version of 'Somewhere Over The Rainbow' and ended up winning the whole competition. There were a load of celebrities in the audience and they gave me a standing ovation, which I was chuffed to bits with. It was absolutely unreal. Plus I got to go and watch Man U play a few times as well.

Whenever I went in for these competitions, I always tried to put my own slant on a song. I like to sing in a soulful way, so for example I might take a jazz song and perform it like Stevie Wonder. I love improvizing and someone once told me I never sing the same song twice. I once sang 'Mack The Knife' in the style of Ray Charles. It's not necessarily the easiest or safest option at a singing competition, but it's always fun.

At times I felt like I was living two separate childhoods and it could be a pretty weird mix. The day after I kissed Britney Spears, and the day following my Old Trafford win, I was back at school in Gloucester. Back in the classroom I didn't talk

looking back,
being jeered
at for kissing
one of the most
beautiful women
in the world …
how bad is that
exactly?!

about my singing much, so if felt like I was leading two different lives.

After my parents separated I lived with my mum, and one day we were reading a copy of the *Stage* magazine. There was an advert in there for the Sylvia Young Theatre School and we were laughing and joking, saying, 'I wonder what that's like? I bet it's a different life!' I'd already got a place at a school called The Crypt in Gloucester, a tough boys' school that concentrates on rugby, and I was thinking, *Oh God, when everyone finds out I sing, it's gonna go down really well!*

The Sylvia Young School offered scholarships, so I thought, *Why not? Let's give it a go.* I wasn't particularly set on

going, but I was interested to see what everyone else in the industry was like. To be honest, at the start I couldn't have cared less about getting in. I suspect Sylvia won't be very pleased to hear me saying that, but that's kinda how I felt. I'd heard of Sylvia Young's because there was a documentary about the school on TV at the time that I'd watched and it had looked quite good – the kids who went there were certainly of a high standard – but seeing them sing and dance on telly is one thing, actually being in an audition next to them is totally different. I'd lived in Gloucester all my life, and was used to going up against local people in competitions, but I didn't know what the standard was like out in the wider world. I just hoped it would be a really good experience and that I'd get to meet Sylvia and maybe she'd give me some advice on how I could improve.

I got through the preliminary auditions and, at the final one, I sang 'Somewhere Over The Rainbow', after which I headed back on my journey home. About half an hour after I'd left, I was at Baker Street Tube station when my mobile rang. It was Sylvia offering me a scholarship.

It was a really good moment in my life and one that will always stand out. I went crazy, jumping up and down so the whole of Baker Street station was like, 'What the hell is that kid on?!' I was happy in Gloucester and I had a place at The Crypt, but there was no way I was going to turn this opportunity down. I know I said that at first I wasn't that set on getting in, and I was more into pop than musical theatre, but once I'd visited the school and met Sylvia – who is an amazing lady – I could see that it would be a brilliant thing to do. So when she phoned and offered me the place, I was chuffed to bits.

Sylvia is *very* to the point, that's what I love about her and that's why we really got on. In the first assembly, she stood there and looked around the room, scanning the faces in front of her. Then she said, 'In this room, three of you will make it.'

I always try to put my
own slant on a song.
I love improvizing

There were about sixty kids standing there in total silence. Then she said, 'I know who those three people are, but things can change if you get a bad attitude or don't work hard. If you get ahead of yourself or complacent you will not make it. That's the message to those three people who I think will make it. To the others, my message is this: be ready to take their place.' We were all like, 'What the … ? This is gonna be interesting!' So no pressure then!

It was a really fascinating place to go to school. I was there from the age of eleven to sixteen. Three days a week it was Science, Maths, English, all the academic stuff, then Thursday and Friday was drama, singing and dance. For the first two years you have to try everything. I tried dancing, but soon realized I was awful, and by the end of Year 11 I went to see Sylvia and said, 'I'm not dancing today!'

She didn't mind because she knew I'd probably just sit in the corner of class not doing anything! She was also very supportive of my passion for pop. That's despite it being a school where almost everyone wants the same thing: a career in musical theatre. Luckily for me, Sylvia didn't seem to mind my pop ambitions!

Sylvia supported me in her own particular way. She would tell me off when I did riffs and vocal ad-libs, saying, 'The younger students will try and copy you. Don't do that. You're a bad influence, Nathan.' That's one of her pet hates: musical theatre students doing R&B. Sorry Sylvia!

There's an agency attached to the school that starts to get the students work throughout their time at the school, and one of the really fun things – or should I say lucrative things – was doing foreign language voice-overs. You'd sit there in a little recording booth speaking really precise English, 'The cat sat on the mat …' It was bizarre but they paid loads, so I did as much as they would give me. Shed-loads in fact!

I was also put in touch with tons of label heads and music industry people, so it was a really good introduction to the business and there were lots of different opportunities to see what people are like. And, of course, they also pointed you in the direction of all sorts of auditions. For one particular audition – for a new band – Sylvia sent every single boy in my year, me included …

Although my childhood home was full of music, I have to be honest and say that for a long time I never really thought about singing in a band. We lived in one of them houses where kids in the street would just knock on the door at all hours and say, 'Can I come in?', or 'Are you gonna come out to play?' And I loved doing both. I recall being out in the garden more than in the house, although I also remember watching absolutely loads of TV while eating crisps! *Power Rangers*, *Biker Mice From Mars*, *Thunderbirds*, anything with baddies to kill. I've got an older brother, Luke, a twin called Tom and a younger brother called Sean, as well as a younger sister called Eleanor, so it's a pretty big family. I was born right in the middle of the summer holidays, on 24 July 1990.

I grew up in Newark in Nottingham. I can't remember our first home, but when I was two we moved to a semi-detached house with a pretty huge garden – it was great considering my dad was just an electrician and Mum didn't work. There was me and my twin brother, my little brother and my big brother in one room, and my mum and dad with my little sister in a baby cot in their room. My little sister was a total beauty then, dead sweet. Grandma and Granddad lived just up the road. That's great int'it?

Mum was basically the head of the family. My dad worked away a lot and he'd ring us at the weekend, but we'd only see him whenever he got back 'cos he travelled loads. He'd only have a weekend back home every now and again, and we loved him for it 'cos he'd always come home with presents, like a little M&M wristwatch or a baseball cap, and we'd go mental. Mum had to do all the disciplining and she was *proper* strict.

Once, when I was dead young, I was having this party and I'd had too many sweets and was going a bit crazy, thinking I was dead hard with me mates. She gave me a right rollicking in front of them all and I was like, *Oh no, for God's sake!* She was the mum round town dragging the kids after her: 'Come on, get here!' At the time I thought she was strict, but now I'm older I realize she's done a cracking job of us, and she's still doing it now.

Mum used to shave our hair over the tiles in the kitchen. We'd grow mops for about six months, then suddenly, overnight, these mop-haired kids would arrive at school with shaved heads, like a flock of sheep. I didn't mind, although Mum always missed bits around the ears, so we'd have to get the scissors and trim them off. That didn't happen to my sister, though!

Me and my twin, Tom, were pretty much best friends. We aren't identical, although when we were together people sometimes had difficulty telling us apart. Back then I was tall but pretty stocky – well, pretty fat really – while Tom was dead little. If I showed you pictures he looks like a little Disney kid, and the cutest thing ever, whereas now he looks like a proper student type. I was just this ball of sweat that used to breathe with my mouth open. He used to call me Jumbo Jay and he was Tiny Tom, and that's how people could tell who was who. It's only looking back that I think, *Oh my God, I was fat!* I was a fat kid and I never even noticed. *Is that me, that huge sweating beast?!*

Me and Tom are still really tight. We were at school together and were dead lairy and cheeky, but we were good kids and we worked hard. At that age we both liked football; in fact, all my family were into it. My dad played football until his knees started to play up, my big brother was captain of his football team and my twin brother was an amazing goalie, even my little sister was in a team. I very quickly fell out of love with football, though, 'cos I was awful. At that age you don't know how good anyone is 'cos you all just run around following the ball. I was just … rubbish.

Perhaps, most unusually, my mum was a brilliant footballer; she was captain of her local team. Mum was a bit of a tomboy; she was loud but just wicked. Even though I didn't

to be honest at
that age it was all
about the dancing

like football I used to love watching her play. They played in this tournament somewhere by a river once, and I remember spending two days catching fish and watching my mum play football; it was this brilliant mini-holiday. I loved all the women that played football, too – all Mum's mates – it was great.

School for us was the Holy Trinity Roman Catholic School in Newark. It was proper holy! There was a church in the car park. We had to do confirmation and we all had our hair cut in the same page-boy curtain style … horrible! School was good, though. I stayed religious for the longest out of all the lads in my family; I kept it going till I was about 15, but I think it was more because my mum liked me going, so I did it for her. You get to a point when your heart's not in it, though. Eventually I stopped going every week, then it'd be every two weeks, then I'd miss the second week 'accidentally on purpose' and soon it faded away altogether.

One of my earliest memories is of a trip to Ireland to see my Aunty Josephine back when I was about six. We went on the ferry, and at that age I couldn't comprehend what this big boat was. I was amazed, I thought I was on a rocket or something, but it was just a ferry! My aunty made us massive breakfasts and I love my food so I went mental. Although I'm vegetarian now, I wasn't back then, so I really enjoyed the

square sausages she gave us. I was completely bowled over. Apart from the square sausages – which made a pretty big impact – she also had a picture of Jesus on her wall and the eyes followed you, they *actually* moved. Me and Tom would crawl up the stairs and see if the eyes would follow us; it was dead creepy. We also had holidays at Butlins, which were great.

Back at school I was the shy one out of me and my brother. In the grand scheme of things, I wasn't a popular kid, but I wasn't annoying or weird either, I was just somewhere in between. I didn't really grab anyone's attention, although at home I was a bit madder.

Primary school was really cushy, but I had a shock when I got to my secondary school. It took an hour and a half to get there, and we were the first kids to be picked up by the school bus and the last ones to be dropped off. We had to get up ridiculously early when it was still dark. I couldn't believe it, I was gutted.

When I was 13, my mum got injured and couldn't play football for a while. I didn't realize then what an important effect her lay-off would have on my life. To keep fit and slim, even though she's tiny – about two stone! – she started going to a tap class with all her mates. She used to drag me along to everything the family did, just to see if I liked something, but I was always rubbish at everything. However, one night I went and watched her tap class and thought, *This is really good!* So I asked if I could learn too.

I didn't want to go to a class where there'd be loads of girls, 'cos at that point I was like, 'Eurrgghh! Girls!' So I asked her for private lessons, but she was like, 'No way. Your brothers don't have private lessons. If you want to go, you can go to this class.' So that's what I did: I started going to the Charlotte Hamilton School of Dance every Thursday. There was only one other lad in the class, and in a way I felt proper awkward, being used to living in a dead loud

my mum started going to a tap class and one night I thought, *this is really good,* so I asked if I could learn too

house with loads of lads running around, but I soon realized that being one of only two boys, I got loads of attention, and I thought, *I can roll with this!*

The class was nothing to do with school, and as far as I knew no one from school went there or knew I was going. I was massively relieved about that 'cos I wasn't sure how people would react if they found out I went to dance classes. Then when I got there on the first night, one of the first people I saw was a girl from school; I was gutted.

Still, I really enjoyed that night. Obviously I couldn't tap yet – I was just trying to hold a position and listen to what was being said – but it felt different. Say with football, I couldn't do it very well, but I knew I wasn't going to get any better either. With tap, I looked down and knew what I was meant to be doing, I just couldn't make my feet do it yet, so I knew I could be good. Very quickly I absolutely loved it and I loved getting better. The girls'd be there in tights and I'd rock up in my trackies and think I was dead hard. It felt wicked.

To be totally honest, at that age I didn't really care about music. I'd been to a few folk concerts with my parents. My first record was by R Kelly and we used to have a Saw Doctors' album on cassette, which we listened to on the way to school every day and knew by heart. Apart from that, I never thought about playing an instrument. I didn't sing, I didn't even know if I could sing – it was all about dancing at that point. Like most families, we loved singing along in the car or at Christmas to *Now That's What I Call Music!*, but at that age you don't relate that to thinking you're good at singing or to the idea of singing as a career. It didn't even cross my mind.
The music I listened to was literally whatever my

I googled 'Auditions' and found two. One was for a circus while the other simply said, 'Wanted: Male Vocalists ...'

parents listened to, which was stuff like The Beautiful South. Mum used to like dancing to Northern Soul, so we had loads of random hits from that era. There was quite a lot of older music around, in fact, I used to watch *Top of the Pops 2* and think that was normal music telly. For a long time I didn't buy music. You did your chores and got money which you spent on sweets … why would you buy a CD?

Back at tap class, I was really getting into it and my teacher, Charlotte Hamilton, was very supportive. She was a really nice woman, very sarcastic and funny. One night she said to Mum, 'Jay's really good, maybe try to get him involved in other classes.' After that, I started doing other forms of dance, too, such as ballet, theatre craft, modern, loads of stuff to make you flexible and versatile. I enjoyed all of it, but tap was my favourite.

In the dinner queue, I'd have my feet flat on the floor, but in my head I'd be going through new dance moves. By the following week I would *always* know the routine. My brain normally got there quite quickly, it was just a case of getting my feet to follow. Dancing really well is a mix of the two – you need to do it with your body as you're being taught the steps. It's all about a *feeling* and imitating that so you recognize the feeling. You can't really see what you look like, even in front of the mirror, so you have to feel what the dance is and then make that feeling happen.

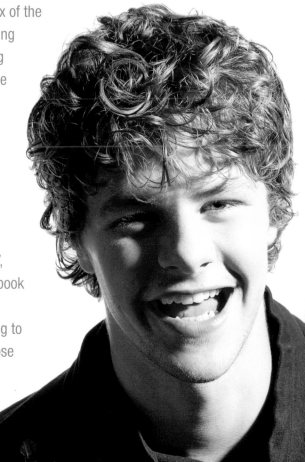

Apart from tap, I used to read a lot. I liked all the Harry Potter books and other fantasy novels. I've always read a lot, but I think that was mainly a lazy thing, 'cos you get to lie down with a book and no one tells you off. If you lie down watching TV, they're like, 'Jay! Sit up!' but if you lie down with a book it's fine 'cos it's 'educational'.

Inevitably the kids at school found out I was going to dance classes and I'd literally get one comment, those two words: 'Billy Elliot!' It didn't bother me though because it was the tiniest bit of stick compared to what I could have got. Plus I'd seen the film, so I knew there could be a happy ending! Anyway, I was proud of my tap. At school they did a dance GCSE, but there was just no way in hell I was gonna do that. I kept under the radar and pretty much got away with it. My friends knew and they were fine with it, some of 'em would even come and see me in the odd show, but mainly my dance was something separate from school.

When it came to choosing what I was going to do after secondary school, there was nothing else that I was really good at or cared about, so I asked if I could go to dance college for three years. There was one not too far away called the Midlands Academy of Dance and Drama and my mum was really up for it. Getting enrolled involved the first proper audition I'd ever done. I had to do two dances, sing and then do a bit of acting. I'd only ever done school plays, so I was absolutely crap at acting, but my singing was OK – I sang Elvis's 'A Little Less Conversation'. Parts of my audition were awful, but then I did my tap at the end and because that was drummed into my head – plus the headmistress loved guys that tap – I got in, thank God.

At first I was a fee-paying student, but while I was at college my mum and dad split up and there was no way they could afford to continue paying for me to go to college. I was waiting tables to help out, but we were still miles short. I owed them anyway because, amazingly, they'd remortgaged their house to get me into college in the first place, which was a massive weight on my shoulders to keep going. In the end I went for an audition in front of a panel and was lucky enough to be awarded an 80 per cent scholarship, so we were sorted, which was obviously a huge relief.

The WANTED

I have to admit, initially my heart wasn't really in it at the dance academy. It felt like work at first, but then as I settled in and got my little circle of mates – the normal lads, not the dramatic ones! – I started to enjoy myself. In the second year I moved in with two lads, Tray and Paul; we lived really close to the city centre for the rest of college and that totally sorted me out. We listened to music a lot and I went to my first proper gig, Muse. I loved every minute of college after that. I started to get heavily into music, either at college when I was dancing or just listening to bands at home, and eventually I found myself singing more and more. Even though my confidence in my vocals was pretty low at first, I began to enjoy it and, just like my early attempts at dancing, I could see myself improving all the time.

In the third year at college they let you start looking for jobs, and I was lucky enough to get a part in the panto *Aladdin* in Inverness. It was my first Christmas away from home and I was earning absolutely amazing money – it was basically a holiday with a few mates in Scotland and the show was pretty fun to do as well. When I got back home, we had a fake Christmas to celebrate. I bought my brother a pair of trainers, my little brother a Celtic jacket, my little sister an iPod, my mum got a digital photo frame and I even bought the whole family a Wii. I was like, *Money SO makes you happy!* Mind you, in return I think I got a belt and pair of earrings … I was a bit gutted about that.

I was feeling really independent and thought this was the start of me being a dancer, but it didn't really happen like that. At the end of each year, the college did a summer showcase and a few people were lucky enough to get an agent. In fact, Tray, Paul and me all did. The agency got me loads of auditions, but none of them seemed to lead to any dance work. Sometimes I'd get really close to the end and then I'd look at the guy next to me and think, *I know I've not got it* … 'cos he'd be like, 28 and ripped and 'seen it all'. I knew I wasn't ready. I didn't look right: I was tall, gangly, not very hip-hop and really geeky.

I kept going but it was very draining, every week doing a couple of auditions and then having to get the train home only to find out a few days or weeks later that it was another 'No'. Some people do that for years before they get anything, but after six months I was pulling my hair out. So instead of waiting for the agency to book me some more of the same stuff, I googled 'Auditions' and found two that looked interesting.

One was for a circus, swinging off wires and all that, while the other advert simply said, 'Wanted: Male Vocalists …'

The WANTED

I absolutely love being in this band, it's amazing. However, when I was a kid, you might be surprised to know that I never thought I'd grow up to be a singer. Back then it was all about football for me; I was mad about it and every day I dreamed of being a professional player.

My story starts in Kildare Road, Swinton, where me mum and dad brought me and my brother Jack up. I've got a huge family. My mum's one of nine and they were all based in Salford; there's loads of 'em! They were always round, all me older cousins, aunties and uncles, so me mum and dad used to throw wicked parties. It was great.

Jack is older than me and the pair of us used to terrorize the house. We were – and still are – best mates. Always fighting and playing football. Anywhere I went I had to have a ball wi' me. Dad first started teaching me to play when I was only three. Back then I just wanted to be a footballer. I was literally never without a football by my side.

My dad's a salesman and he's also a football coach for underprivileged kids, while my mum is a medicine consultant for doctors. Me nan and granddad live just up the road (we all still live really close to each other). A massive part of my upbringing was me nan and granddad; they moved up from Essex when I was born to

when I was growing
up music was playing
all the time ... I loved it,
but music was never
my ambition as a kid

help my parents out and I used to be round theirs every night. That's where I learned to play football, on the field right by their house.

When I was seven, me mum and dad separated. It was a bit weird after that: there weren't as many parties and it was a lot quieter round our house. Dad only moved a mile away, so I still saw him all the time. I spent alternate nights with each of them – Monday was Dad, Tuesday was Mum, etc. – so to be fair to them, the separation didn't affect me too much. There was an initial period when it was a bit awkward, but it soon picked up again. It was a bad time for me mum and dad, but Jack and I never stopped gooning about!

When I was 13, Mum, Jack and I moved into a huge new house in the middle of the estate … now that *was* a party house! It was on its own in the middle of this massive patch of grass and we'd have mad parties all the time. The house would be so rammed with people you'd look round and hardly know anyone there at times!

The WANTED

'All right, mate, do you mind if we come in and join your party?'

'Nah, not at all, come in!'

I was a bit of a terror at primary school. I was born on 6 September 1988, which made me one of the oldest in the school year, and I went to Broad Oak Primary School in Manchester. I was a bit naughty and was always chasing girls – same as now really! – playing football and getting up to mischief with me mates Kev and Paul; the three of us were really tight. I loved primary school; it was brilliant. My brother went there too, and to this day some of my closest friends are from Broad Oak. Sometimes I wish I could go back … it was great!

My head teacher, Mr Connelly, was amazing, but I don't know if he'd remember me quite so fondly. I just liked messing about and found being Jack the Lad more entertaining than doing maths or science. I was never very academic and got sent out of class quite a lot. I used to have to go and stand by the fire extinguisher facing the wall.

I was lucky though because my parents were quite relaxed; it wasn't that they didn't care – far from it – but what they wanted more than anything was

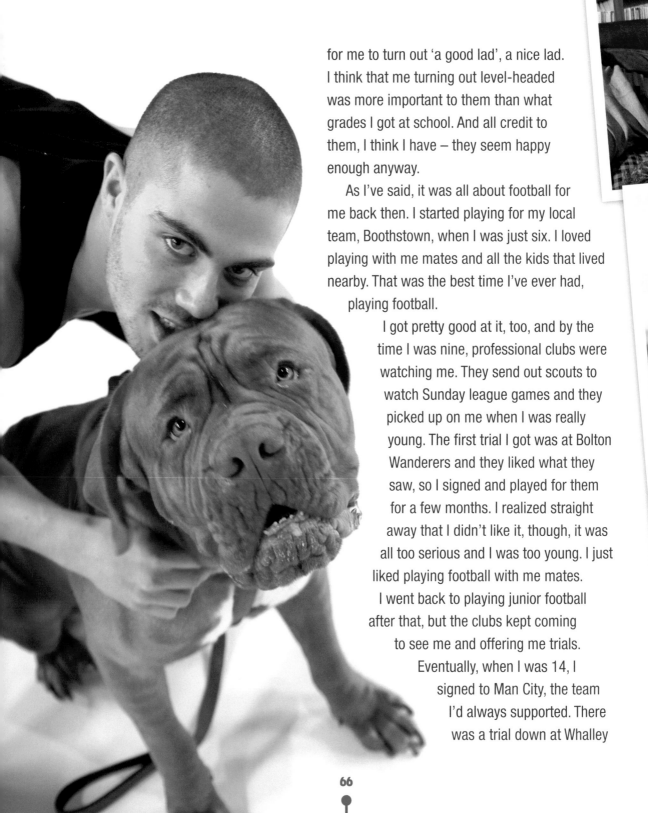

for me to turn out 'a good lad', a nice lad. I think that me turning out level-headed was more important to them than what grades I got at school. And all credit to them, I think I have – they seem happy enough anyway.

As I've said, it was all about football for me back then. I started playing for my local team, Boothstown, when I was just six. I loved playing with me mates and all the kids that lived nearby. That was the best time I've ever had, playing football.

I got pretty good at it, too, and by the time I was nine, professional clubs were watching me. They send out scouts to watch Sunday league games and they picked up on me when I was really young. The first trial I got was at Bolton Wanderers and they liked what they saw, so I signed and played for them for a few months. I realized straight away that I didn't like it, though, it was all too serious and I was too young. I just liked playing football with me mates. I went back to playing junior football after that, but the clubs kept coming to see me and offering me trials. Eventually, when I was 14, I signed to Man City, the team I'd always supported. There was a trial down at Whalley

Range High School. We'd just been on holiday to Barcelona and while we were there I saw these incredible new football boots. I was like, 'Dad, you gotta get me these!' but he said, 'You can't have 'em, you'll break your ankle in them, they're just a little piece of rubber!' Anyway, I pestered him until he bought them for me.

At the trial for Man City, I wore these brand-new boots and after about five minutes they were rubbing me terrible. I played on, though, but eventually had to come off 'cos the boots were killing me and I had this big flap of skin hanging off me foot. I lied and told me dad I'd twisted me ankle. Luckily, Man City offered me a one-year deal right there and then at the side of the pitch, but then they said, 'Right, let's get a physio to look at your twisted ankle'!

Being on their books as a schoolboy player was a fantastic opportunity to establish myself and hopefully get offered a senior professional playing contract when I was old enough. Being offered that deal with Man City – *my* team – was an amazing feeling. For the first time I thought to myself, *Right, you know what? I'm gonna do this, I'm gonna really try*. By this point, I'd spent the best part of eight years in junior football Sunday leagues. I'd had the best time and won a load of trophies with me team, Boothstown; we were a top side, but now it was time to go for it.

In the end, though, my time at City wasn't what I thought it would be. They had amazing facilities, of course, but the longer it went on, the more I didn't like some of the other lads' attitudes. It sometimes seemed like it was all about 'me, me, me'; it didn't feel like a team game and I didn't like that side of it. When Boothstown played, I'd want the *team* to win, I didn't want *me* to win, whereas at City it could feel like eleven individuals. Then I snapped my hamstring and during the four-month injury lay-off I thought, *Do you know what? I don't even like it there …*

I hadn't lost interest in football, though, so I left and played for Blackburn Rovers for six months, where I had a great time. During that period, Boothstown asked me back for one more match.

what my
parents
wanted
more than
anything
was for me
to turn out
'a good lad'

I came on as a sub when we were winning 3–2, and after about five minutes I tackled their keeper and, next thing I know I was sent off. It was a shocking decision. Worse still, after the resulting free kick the other team went up the pitch, equalized, then went on to win the match on penalties. Boothstown never asked me back again!

After that I played for England Independent School Boys, getting five or six caps and scoring on my debut. I had trials for Manchester United, and signed for Oldham FC, where I played for two years and loved every minute. What I didn't know then was that my time in football was coming to an end.

All the while I was playing football for these other clubs, my school – Bolton High School – wasn't as supportive as I'd have liked. I think they didn't like you playing for teams outside the school. I had a brilliant English teacher, Mr Holland, but other than that I didn't enjoy it much. To be fair, I was lazy in lessons. My brother, who was also at the school, was really academic, while I was always chasing girls and being one of the lads.

Back at Oldham FC I was getting pretty serious and playing really well, scoring every week. I was proper on top of me game at that point and I genuinely thought I could make it as a professional footballer. Then, in the pre-match warm-up for an England trial, I snapped my hip flexor, which is a very serious injury. I didn't tell anyone and just sat on the bench waiting to be called. They brought me on and I touched the ball once, hitting a volley that flew into the top corner. It was one of the best goals of me life, but I could hardly walk afterwards. I knew it was a bad injury, but what I didn't know then was that my football career could be under threat.

Virtually no one in our family has a talent for music or a musical career. One of me uncles is a singer and does the pubs' and clubs' circuit, but apart from that it's just me. Oh, and me nan can sing as well (in fact she used to do the clubs in London). However, when I was growing up music was playing all the time – mainly Sinatra and Dean Martin, plus me nan used to play loads of jazz. I can remember hearing jazz playing in her house while I lay in bed. I loved it, but music was never my ambition as a kid.

While I was injured I decided to audition for *The X Factor*. My brother had tried out for *Pop Idol* but completely messed up his audition and didn't get through. Then the next year it became *The X Factor* and I heard about this open audition for over 16s – I was 16 at the time. I told me dad I was doing it and he was like, 'All right, if you wanna go for it, go for it, fair enough.' I'd always listened to music – my first album was *Off The Wall* by Michael Jackson and my first ever concert was Oasis – but it wasn't something I wanted to do for a living. I only went to the audition 'cos our Jack'd had a go! My parents always backed me when I wanted to try something, so when *The X Factor* was in town, Dad dropped me off at about half six in the morning. There was a two-mile queue and it took me eight hours before I saw a producer. I sang and they put me straight through. Brilliant!

The only problem was I had my History GCSE exam that afternoon, so I ran back to school, did

the exam, then ran back to the auditions. This time it was in front of the judges and I got a 'Yes' from Louis, Sharon and Simon – Simon even compared me to a young Robbie Williams – *and* it was all on the telly. I couldn't believe it. I hadn't really sung before, and as I said, I only went because of Jack. I was so excited; I'd always watched the show round me dad's on a Saturday night with a kebab.

It was boot camp in London a few weeks later. I got there and started chatting to this guy and he was a sound lad, so I hung about with him and we had a coupla pints, then a couple turned into quite a few more, and then there was a party with these girls and we ended up staying awake until 7 a.m. The problem was, I had to leave for the theatre at 7.15 and I hadn't slept at all!

When I got up in front of the judges I had to sing 'Unchained Melody', but hardly a word came out. I was awful. Worse still, Shayne Ward sang right before me and he was brilliant. Louis sent me home. The funny thing is, though, I didn't feel down 'cos I never expected to get anywhere – I'd had a great time and now I'd got the buzz of singing and performing in my head.

Despite my experience on *The X Factor*, my reality at this point was still football. Even though I'd recovered from my hip injury, I'd lost a few yards of pace on the pitch and just couldn't compete the way I used to. It became much harder work. Oldham FC released me soon afterwards and then I got picked up by Preston on a trial. But it just wasn't the same. I was proper starting to like going out, and the whole social side of being a teenager was much more appealing to me than all those early starts and having to train four times a week. By now, one of the issues with my football was that I liked to party. By the time I got to 16 I was pretty much partying all the time. We used to have some wild house parties at me mum's house when she was away with work – if only she'd been there! We'd all have a great time and me mates would get me up on their shoulders at the end of the night, everyone would be cheering me name and I felt like the Godfather. That was probably part of my downfall!

I'd had a great time
and now I'd got the
buzz of singing and
performing in my head

Don't get me wrong, I wasn't a total party animal. I love a brew at me nan's house and I still go round and mow the lawn and sweep the leaves up for me granddad – if I didn't, he'd give me a backhander, even now!

I remember sitting at me mum's house one afternoon waiting for Dad to pick me up at 6 o'clock for a training session. I'd just got in from school and I thought to myself, *I don't want to do this any more*. I rang me dad and said, 'I don't want to do it any more.' He said, 'What do you mean?' And I replied, 'I don't want to be a footballer any more.' It was tough for everyone, especially me dad and granddad, 'cos they'd taken me everywhere, all around the country and even Europe, so for them the news was a massive shock. I hid from me dad for a couple of months and didn't see him much – it wasn't deliberate, but mentally I couldn't face him. Even thinking about it now is uncomfortable 'cos he'd put so much work into helping me become a footballer.

My family is incredible and I feel very lucky to have had their support whatever decisions I've made. I don't regret quitting football for one minute; in fact my only regrets are that I never met two very special people in my family: my Nana Mary and Uncle Dave. Nana Mary was the my mum's mum, who was the head of the family and who unfortunately died of cancer before I was born, while Uncle Dave was my dad's brother, who died suddenly of a heart attack at only thirty-two. He was my dad's best friend.

After I quit football I started doing a sports diploma at college, but I was just bumming around really. I hardly ever turned up and was messing about with girls again. Around the same time one of my friends (Jonny Kerrigan 'The Gentle Giant'), who was only 18,

died of cancer, which put me in a pretty bad spot. There were a few things happening at once, and the end result was that I was struggling to get focused and back on track for quite a while. I just couldn't seem to get sorted.

It must have been frustrating for me mum and dad to see, and they were worried about what I was going to do next. At one point I thought I'd take up an apprenticeship, but I didn't really know what I wanted to do. I just wanted to be a 16 year old who didn't have any worries.

I'd started smoking and having a few beers, and I still wasn't turning up for college, so after six months they threw me out. I was 17 and didn't have a clue what I wanted to do.

One thing I kept thinking about was *The X Factor* audition. It had made a really big impact on me, more than anything else at the time. With football taking a back seat, I started to think about a life in music instead. I'd always loved Swing music and around this time I did a couple of gigs with a friend of mine, Cole Page, who's a big Swing singer in Manchester. I also started doing a bit of singing on me own here and there, but I still didn't know where I was gonna go in terms of a career. I left college, then in the February I got a phone call from a music manager who'd seen *The X Factor*, asking me to audition for a new band that was being put together. I went down to the Sadler's Wells Theatre in London, and after a few weeks of auditions I was offered a place in a band that was going to be called Avenue.

I moved straight down to London into this lovely flat with the other lads in the band. We had a great time and rehearsed constantly. Then, as most people know, we went on *The X Factor* and got all the way through to the live final. Then the papers got hold of the fact that we already had a manager, so Louis called us in for a meeting and told us we were disqualified as that was against the rules. I was absolutely gutted, tearful and devastated. We had to just take it on the chin, which was difficult, but at the end of the day that's life and you can't complain.

We continued as Avenue for a while, but a few of us could tell it wasn't happening. Then I got a phone call from Ashley Tabor from Global, the man who gave me my first break in the music industry. He asked me to come down to London to meet the team behind what was to be a brand-new band …

The WANTED

I guess this whole crazy thing started when my father and mother pushed my elder sister Hazel to sing a bit of karaoke. It turned out she was really good and she started doing local competitions, singing as much as she could. The local community was really supportive and she kept doing really well. In fact, the first concert I ever went to was my sister's! Eventually she joined a band called Dove and later went on to get through to the final of *Pop Stars: The Rivals*. Meanwhile, my other sister Gayle became a well-known model in Ireland and my brother David joined a boy band called Zoo, which enjoyed some success and even toured around Ireland and parts of the UK. So I guess music and entertainment was just in our family.

Me mam loved to sing, she wasn't a professional singer but she loved to sing all the old music by artists such as Dionne Warwick. My father loved to listen to music: Lionel Richie and all the Motown stars, Jackson 5, Michael Jackson (my first record was by the Jackson 5), that kind of era. That's where my love of that amazing music comes from, 'cos my parents and sisters and brothers were listening to it constantly. I'm really glad that I heard all that older music because those performers were *amazing*. They'd just stand in a recording studio and sing the song, no Auto-Tuning, no multiple takes, they'd just sing everything straight off. And they used to perform so much, I really admire that, they were performing artists rather than recording artists, and they worked incredibly hard at playing live. That made a big impact on me when I was young and it's something I've always aspired to.

It wasn't common to see a family of Asians in Dublin when I was a little kid. I come from a

I filled up my days with playing and listening to music

large family of eight children. I'm the youngest with my twin brother Kumar. Nowadays Dublin is a very multi-cultural city, but back then it wasn't the case. It's a long story how we came to settle in Dublin. My grandfather was a soldier in the ex-English colony of Sri Lanka, and he met and married my Malaysian grandmother. My dad was born while they were living in Singapore. Dad himself grew up to be a sailor and travelled all over the world. He met me mam in London one time, and that's where it all began. It's a really romantic story because they then met six times over six months – each time for a whole week – fell in love and at the end of that period he proposed to her!

At the time Mam was working in a print factory, but after suffering a bad injury to her hand in a work accident, she flew out to Singapore with Dad and they got married in a Hindu temple.

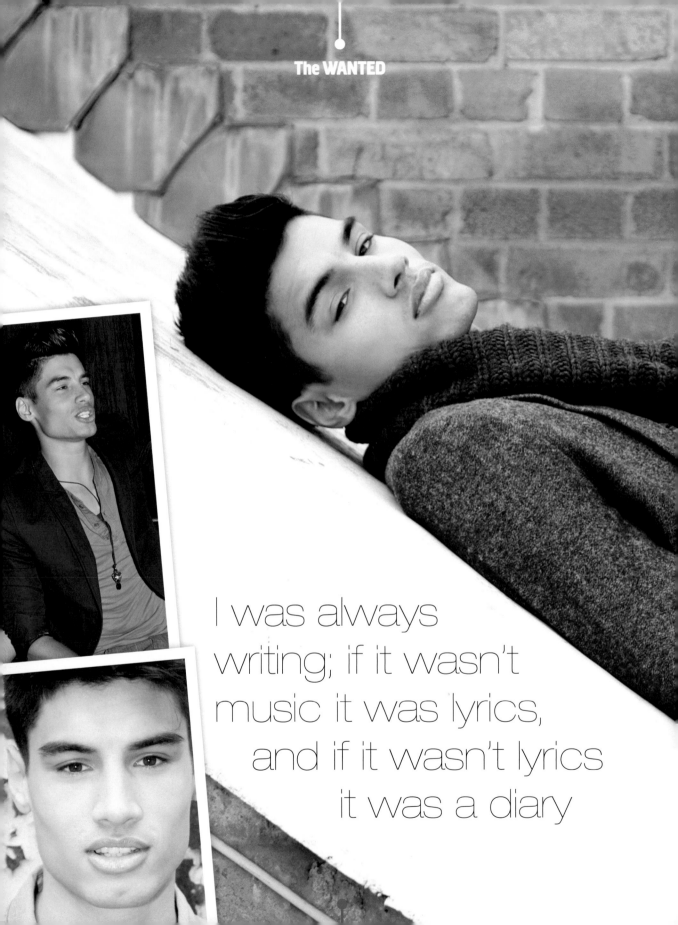

I was always writing; if it wasn't music it was lyrics, and if it wasn't lyrics it was a diary

However, after a few months there she couldn't hack the heat – 'cos she's pale and ginger with freckles – so they came back to Dublin to live and raise kids. I was a winter baby, born on 16 November 1988.

My father passed away when I was only five, so my mam raised all eight of us alone in a house in Dublin. It was obviously incredibly tough for her, but our shared experiences made us come together even more as a family and we definitely grew stronger because of it – I think so anyway. I always refer back to my family, we are very close.

We had the third biggest house on our road, with a kitchen extension, a sitting room and a second sitting room. But with six boys and two girls in the family, we needed a lot of space! My mam bought three bunk beds for us lads, so we had one room between six boys – we all used to fight and laugh and share stories about girls in there. As we got bigger, it wasn't enough space for six growing lads, so Mam built a dividing wall in the second sitting room

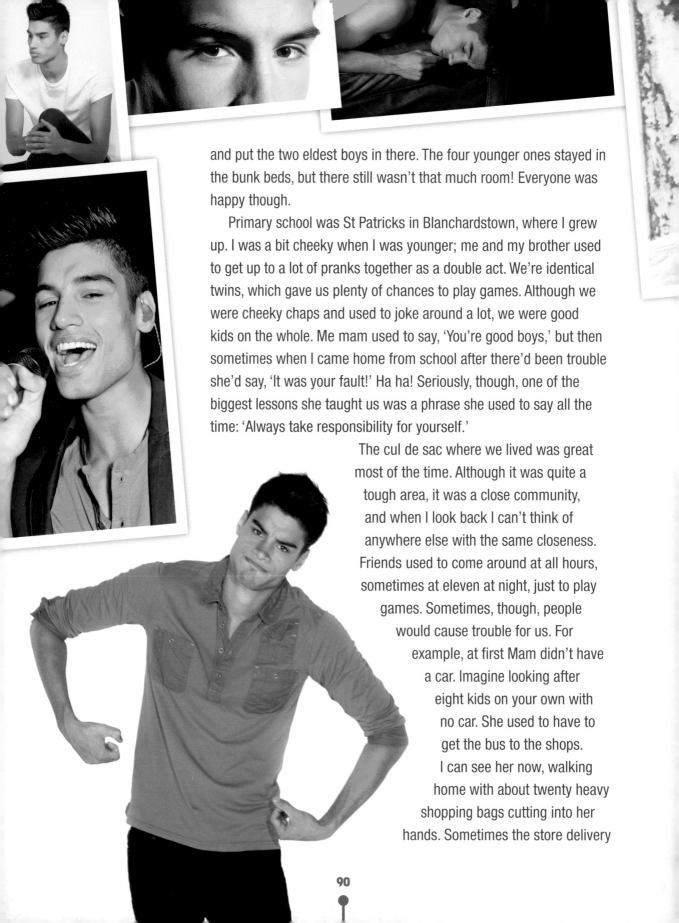

and put the two eldest boys in there. The four younger ones stayed in the bunk beds, but there still wasn't that much room! Everyone was happy though.

Primary school was St Patricks in Blanchardstown, where I grew up. I was a bit cheeky when I was younger; me and my brother used to get up to a lot of pranks together as a double act. We're identical twins, which gave us plenty of chances to play games. Although we were cheeky chaps and used to joke around a lot, we were good kids on the whole. Me mam used to say, 'You're good boys,' but then sometimes when I came home from school after there'd been trouble she'd say, 'It was your fault!' Ha ha! Seriously, though, one of the biggest lessons she taught us was a phrase she used to say all the time: 'Always take responsibility for yourself.'

The cul de sac where we lived was great most of the time. Although it was quite a tough area, it was a close community, and when I look back I can't think of anywhere else with the same closeness. Friends used to come around at all hours, sometimes at eleven at night, just to play games. Sometimes, though, people would cause trouble for us. For example, at first Mam didn't have a car. Imagine looking after eight kids on your own with no car. She used to have to get the bus to the shops. I can see her now, walking home with about twenty heavy shopping bags cutting into her hands. Sometimes the store delivery

man would give her a lift home, but other times she had a long walk back. One day me mam went to a clairvoyant and was told that Dad would've wanted her to buy a car to make her life easier, so that's what she did. Once she had a car it made a big difference, but after only a month someone stole it. Other times trouble came from people who didn't like the family and who smashed the back windows and stuff. Things like that just made me mam want to move away. She worked so hard to look after us and she thought there would be a better life for us in the country, like a lot of people do.

I did my first year in Blanchardstown Secondary School, but then we moved out to the country to a really nice house. Although we'd had some trouble at our old house, it was tough to move away 'cos all me mates were back in Dublin and it had been a really friendly place to live most of the time. At times our new school was tough for a few reasons. Firstly, everyone knew us because of my sisters being in the public eye. One was a pop star and one was a model so, understandably, we stood out. We were always 'that family from Blanchardstown'. That was fine, though, because we were very proud of my sisters. Another reason things were tough wasn't so good. There we were, four brown kids with Dublin city accents turning up at a country school – the only brown kids in a school full of white children. There was discrimination and sometimes it got a bit racist. I used to get bullied an' all. In the beginning, you hear the comments and think, *No, he's not … does he mean that?* Some kids were quite nasty at times.

It wasn't just our skin, though, we were the new boys from out of town. At times you just wanted to go home and cry and say it's not fair, but me mam was brilliant. She was from a family of fifteen herself and just used to say, 'You are, you know, from a very big family, you've got lots of aunties and uncles all over Dublin; they're everywhere. Why are they calling you names? You could be their cousin for all they know.' That always cheered us up. Then she'd say, 'They're being ignorant, you boys just keep your heads high. Keep on doing what you do.'

Even though there were a few tough times in the country when I was growing up, I still love going back to visit. Mam's got a beautiful house by a forest and a lake and she's done it all up so nicely. She was such a brilliant mother and when I look back and think how hard it must have been for her, I can't believe the work and love she put into us kids.

By my early teens, I really got into my music. My brother and I were in the school choir and we sang twice a week, with big performances at Easter, special Masses, Christmas and stuff like that. As we got a little older, we had to help teach the younger kids coming through.

Almost straight away I discovered the guitar too – or rather, my brother's guitar. He was learning guitar and inevitably I picked it up a few times and had a go too. Eventually I picked up a few chords and after that I just loved it. He used to listen to a really broad range of music – The Eagles, U2, Take That – he'd buy music books and learn the chords, then we'd sit there and play acoustic versions of all the songs we liked to each other. Looking back, I began singing and playing guitar as soon as I started listening to music, and I went on to get my first guitar for Christmas when I was sixteen. The three things happened pretty much at the same time.

It seemed natural to me to play and write my own stuff rather than just listen to other people's music. I was always writing; if it wasn't music it was lyrics, and if it wasn't lyrics, it was a diary. I kept a detailed diary for years and years – although me mam's not getting to read it! I love writing; it's something I do all the time. I learned a lot about that from my sisters, who were always writing stuff, and my brother Daniel, who was another big influence on my writing. He got an A Honours in English, and he's really good with words and songwriting. He gave me a passion for thinking about what I write, keeping diaries and using my words. Whenever I have

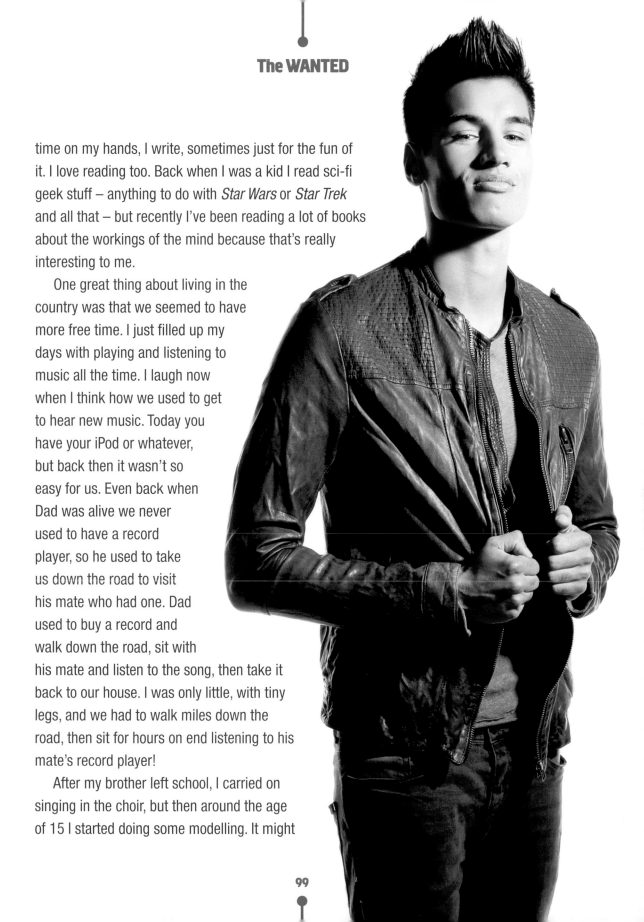

time on my hands, I write, sometimes just for the fun of it. I love reading too. Back when I was a kid I read sci-fi geek stuff – anything to do with *Star Wars* or *Star Trek* and all that – but recently I've been reading a lot of books about the workings of the mind because that's really interesting to me.

One great thing about living in the country was that we seemed to have more free time. I just filled up my days with playing and listening to music all the time. I laugh now when I think how we used to get to hear new music. Today you have your iPod or whatever, but back then it wasn't so easy for us. Even back when Dad was alive we never used to have a record player, so he used to take us down the road to visit his mate who had one. Dad used to buy a record and walk down the road, sit with his mate and listen to the song, then take it back to our house. I was only little, with tiny legs, and we had to walk miles down the road, then sit for hours on end listening to his mate's record player!

After my brother left school, I carried on singing in the choir, but then around the age of 15 I started doing some modelling. It might

me mam loved to sing,
and my dad loved
listening to music –
that's where my love
of music comes from

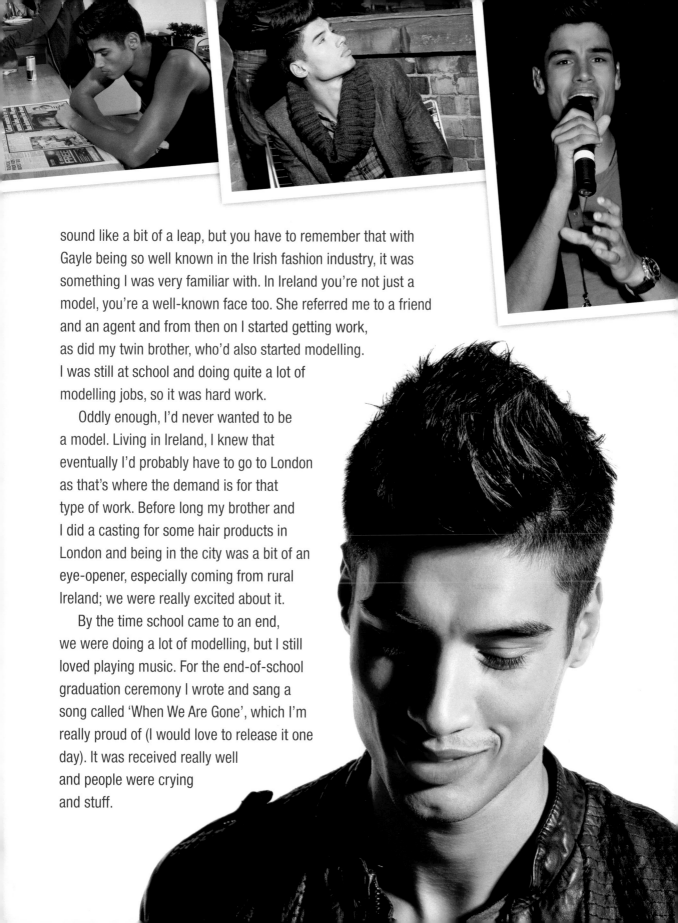

sound like a bit of a leap, but you have to remember that with Gayle being so well known in the Irish fashion industry, it was something I was very familiar with. In Ireland you're not just a model, you're a well-known face too. She referred me to a friend and an agent and from then on I started getting work, as did my twin brother, who'd also started modelling. I was still at school and doing quite a lot of modelling jobs, so it was hard work.

Oddly enough, I'd never wanted to be a model. Living in Ireland, I knew that eventually I'd probably have to go to London as that's where the demand is for that type of work. Before long my brother and I did a casting for some hair products in London and being in the city was a bit of an eye-opener, especially coming from rural Ireland; we were really excited about it.

By the time school came to an end, we were doing a lot of modelling, but I still loved playing music. For the end-of-school graduation ceremony I wrote and sang a song called 'When We Are Gone', which I'm really proud of (I would love to release it one day). It was received really well and people were crying and stuff.

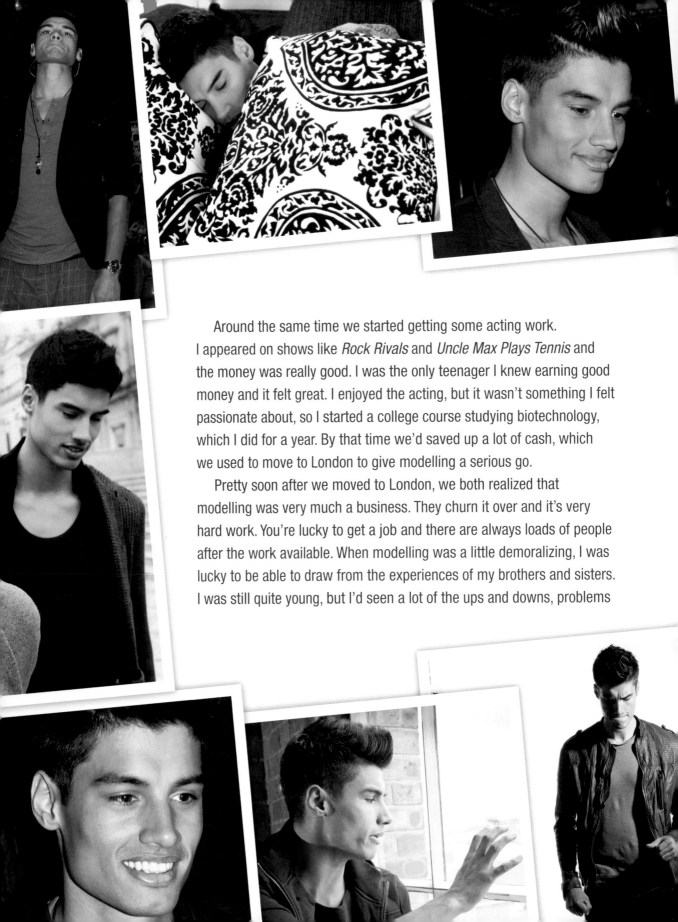

Around the same time we started getting some acting work. I appeared on shows like *Rock Rivals* and *Uncle Max Plays Tennis* and the money was really good. I was the only teenager I knew earning good money and it felt great. I enjoyed the acting, but it wasn't something I felt passionate about, so I started a college course studying biotechnology, which I did for a year. By that time we'd saved up a lot of cash, which we used to move to London to give modelling a serious go.

Pretty soon after we moved to London, we both realized that modelling was very much a business. They churn it over and it's very hard work. You're lucky to get a job and there are always loads of people after the work available. When modelling was a little demoralizing, I was lucky to be able to draw from the experiences of my brothers and sisters. I was still quite young, but I'd seen a lot of the ups and downs, problems

and obstacles in both the music and modelling business, so I kind of knew what to expect.

However, I was starting to realize that to really make it as a model I needed to give it more focus than I was willing to. Don't get me wrong, I got some good jobs, I was with the agency Storm and worked for Armani, Gareth Pugh, G-Star and all that stuff, but the work was very on and off, and there was no structure. I like having a pay cheque at the end of the week, but with modelling you never have that, so I wanted to try something different.

Meanwhile, my brother Trevor really wanted to get into music, and he came across an audition, which he told me and Kumar about. We were already living in London because of our modelling, so Trevor flew over and joined us for this audition, which was to be in a new band …

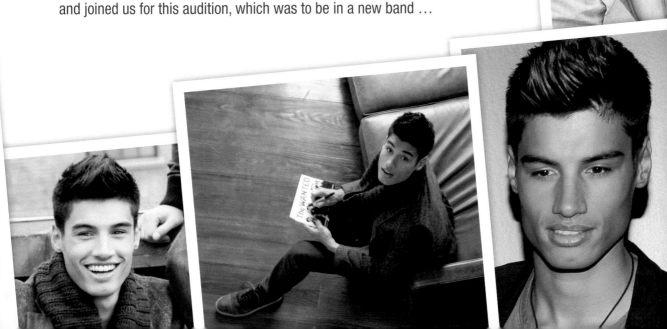

When I were a kid, I was too busy getting into all sorts of scrapes to think about a future in music. I was so in the wars, it were ridiculous! I pretty much drove Mum mad at times, I were that bad. *So* hyperactive. After school I would go out pretty much every day, I never used to bring people round. It's not that I didn't like being in the house, I'm just an outdoor kinda person, so I would always be out with me mates in the street. I always used to be on me bike, falling off, running through patio windows, random stuff! That's why I've got various scars on my face, battle wounds!

I'm the oldest in the band, born a couple of months before Max on 4 August 1988. I was lucky enough to grow up in a really stable home. Me mum and dad didn't have a lot of money but they always tried to make me and my brother feel as comfortable as possible. We lived in a cul de sac; it wasn't the best area in the world, but it certainly wasn't the worst.

The WANTED

I was comfortable as a kid, it was actually a really nice place to grow up. My mum and dad literally gave me everything they could afford. When I look back now, if I'd ask for something at Christmas and birthdays, they would strive to get it. They'd always get us the best thing they could: bikes and PlayStations, the usual stuff. I know now that they couldn't really afford it. Me mum used to work nights as a weaver in a mill and Dad was a cutter in a factory. That's what they needed to do just to get the money in. They'd try somehow to buy us this stuff we wanted and I *so* appreciate that they did.

I have been brought up in a loving family, and even though when you are a kid you sometimes think, *I've not got this and I've not got that*, when you get older you realize that it's the small things that count more than the material things. They just wanted me to have a life that they never had when they were kids.

I absolutely loved my primary school – St Brendan's in Bolton – and I've got really good memories of that time. There were only 18 people in our year, so we were really tight as a group. The teachers were amazing: Mrs Thornton were the head teacher and although she was strict she was brilliant and instilled that discipline into you. Well, she tried! I was *really* naughty as a kid, I used to get sent out every dinner time for chucking food about or causing some sort of disturbance. I used to get in fights about who was the hardest in school and that kind of thing. One teacher had a particular way of punishing you – I laugh when I think of it now – they had these little round bins in class and this teacher would make you stand in the bin. 'Thomas, go and stand in the bin.' Isn't that against my human rights?! It's so funny looking back, but I wouldn't change primary school for the world.

Secondary school was a bit different. To be fair, I was still quite naughty at secondary. I used to turn up all the time – my attendance was second to none – but all my report cards were like, 'Thomas is distracting all the other pupils in the class.' I could never sit still and

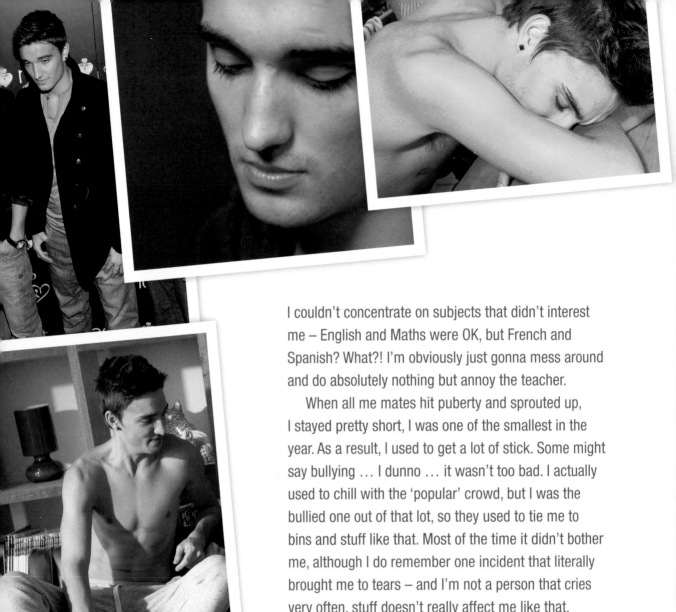

I couldn't concentrate on subjects that didn't interest me – English and Maths were OK, but French and Spanish? What?! I'm obviously just gonna mess around and do absolutely nothing but annoy the teacher.

When all me mates hit puberty and sprouted up, I stayed pretty short, I was one of the smallest in the year. As a result, I used to get a lot of stick. Some might say bullying … I dunno … it wasn't too bad. I actually used to chill with the 'popular' crowd, but I was the bullied one out of that lot, so they used to tie me to bins and stuff like that. Most of the time it didn't bother me, although I do remember one incident that literally brought me to tears – and I'm not a person that cries very often, stuff doesn't really affect me like that.

It was Year 11 and they nicked my school bag with all my GCSE notes in it and hid it from me. I couldn't find it for about a week, and when I eventually did, they'd chucked it over onto the cricket pitch. By the time I'd actually found it all me notes had leaked in the rain and I couldn't read a word. I went home and cried me eyes out to my mum. After that I kinda got into a new crowd, some of the lads I'd been to primary school with in fact, and I distanced myself from the popular gang. I chilled with this nicer bunch of lads for the last

when I were a kid, I was too busy getting into scrapes to think about a future in music

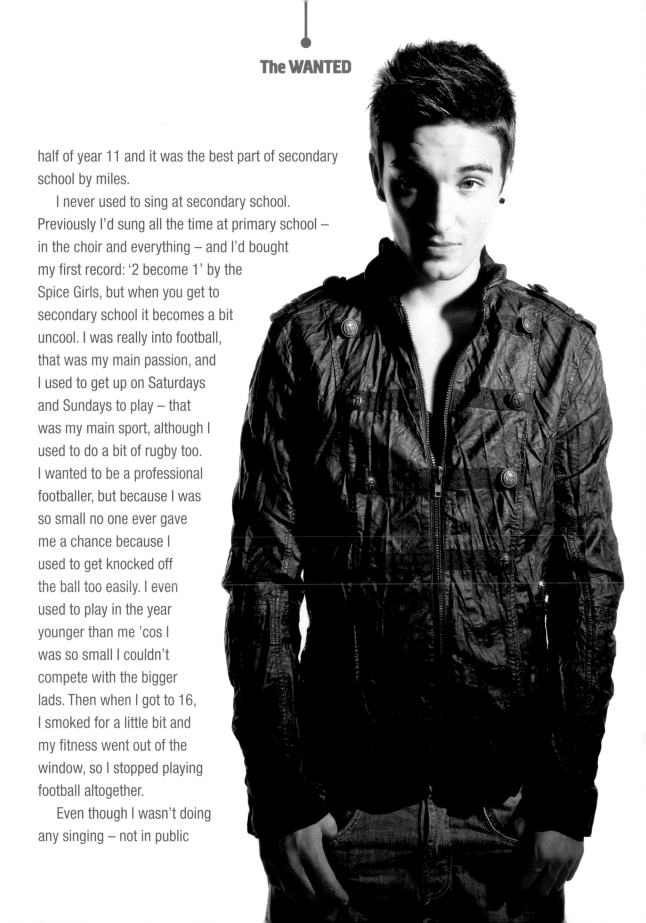

half of year 11 and it was the best part of secondary school by miles.

I never used to sing at secondary school. Previously I'd sung all the time at primary school – in the choir and everything – and I'd bought my first record: '2 become 1' by the Spice Girls, but when you get to secondary school it becomes a bit uncool. I was really into football, that was my main passion, and I used to get up on Saturdays and Sundays to play – that was my main sport, although I used to do a bit of rugby too. I wanted to be a professional footballer, but because I was so small no one ever gave me a chance because I used to get knocked off the ball too easily. I even used to play in the year younger than me 'cos I was so small I couldn't compete with the bigger lads. Then when I got to 16, I smoked for a little bit and my fitness went out of the window, so I stopped playing football altogether.

Even though I wasn't doing any singing – not in public

anyway – I put myself forward to perform at the end-of-year 'Record of Achievement' ceremony, *in front of the whole school year*. To this day I don't know why. On the night I was absolutely petrified. It was the first time I'd sung in public in six years and I was stood there behind this mic with my heart thumping out of my chest. I were like, 'I am proper nervous here!' But I sang and loads of people came up after and said I was really good. That was the turning point – people at school coming up to me and praising me – that's what made me question whether academic work was the right thing for me. I just remember thinking that night, *Singing is for me …*

By the time I got to sixth form, I'd grown a fair bit and had a lot more presence about me, but I didn't really knuckle down there either. I started doing Physics, Psychology and English Literature and Language. But then after only six weeks of doing Physics, we did a test and I got zero out of sixty! I was like, *I don't think Physics is for me, this definitely isn't my subject!* I took up Geography instead, but eventually they got fed up with me and kicked me out, after which I went to another college down the road. When you get a reputation for being trouble in one school it's hard to shake off. It follows you into sixth form too; they all know who you are and they hold it against you. By this point I was like, *I'm not too sure if education is for me.*

What I definitely did want was to play guitar. I first picked up a guitar aged 16, just before sixth form. I'd started listening to the likes of Oasis, the Manics, Blur,

Radiohead and people like that mainly because that's what my brother listened to. He's been a big influence on me musically. (The rockier side of music has always been a favourite and my first gig was a Bolton rock band called Them Bones). My brother used to play along to these songs and one time I went into his bedroom when he weren't there – he'd kill me if he found out … and he will now! – and started playing on his guitar. I couldn't play obviously, but I *really* enjoyed it, so I asked Mum to get me a guitar. My parents were really into their music. My dad sees himself as a bit of a singer and he probably could've been one, but back then he didn't know how to go about pursuing it as a career. It's wasted talent really. I fully understand why people go in for *The X Factor*, even though I'm not sure it's necessarily the best way to go career-wise, because, like my dad, a lot of people have nowhere else to turn.

Eventually I got this rubbish cheap acoustic guitar for 150 quid, something that I really appreciate me mum and dad did for me. It could have just been one of them things, 150 quid for something I'd get bored of in a coupla weeks. 'Wonderwall' was the first song I learned on guitar and to this day it's one of

as soon as I picked up
my brother's guitar, that
was all I wanted to do

my all-time favourites. Sneaking into my brother's room and strumming away on his guitar really ignited my passion for music, and over the next year I played guitar constantly.

In 2004, when I was still just 16, I auditioned for *The X Factor*. Not a good experience! You have to go through three rounds before you meet the judges – Simon and all that – and there are loads of preliminary rounds beforehand. I sang 'Flying Without Wings' by Westlife, which was probably a bad choice because it's quite a big song and everyone sings it. I just thought, *I'm gonna give it a whirl. The X Factor* was quite new at the time and I felt I had nowhere else to turn. I wanted to push myself as a singer, but there were no other avenues open to me.

In the end I didn't get through and I didn't get on the cameras. They said no. I'm thankful I wasn't filmed, though – because rejections like that can be hard to shake off – I was absolutely gutted at the time. The whole experience dented my confidence massively, and for about six months after that I hardly sang at all. I just kept thinking, *If the producers of* The X Factor *don't think I'm good enough, then there must be something wrong.*

I still wasn't enjoying education, but coming from Bolton – even though it's quite a big place – there weren't many opportunities to pursue music. As a result, I did my second year of A levels, and when the exams came along I failed them. Bizarrely, though, I still got into university. I had been given an unconditional offer from Manchester Met, which, amazingly, meant there was a place for me no matter what results I got. This meant I didn't have to do any work, so I was like, BRILLIANT! I was on holiday in Bulgaria with my ex-girlfriend when the results came out, and my dad rang up: 'Thomas, you've failed!' I was like, 'Gutted!' But because of the unconditional offer, the place was still open for me.

that was the turning point, I remember thinking that night, *Singing is for me*

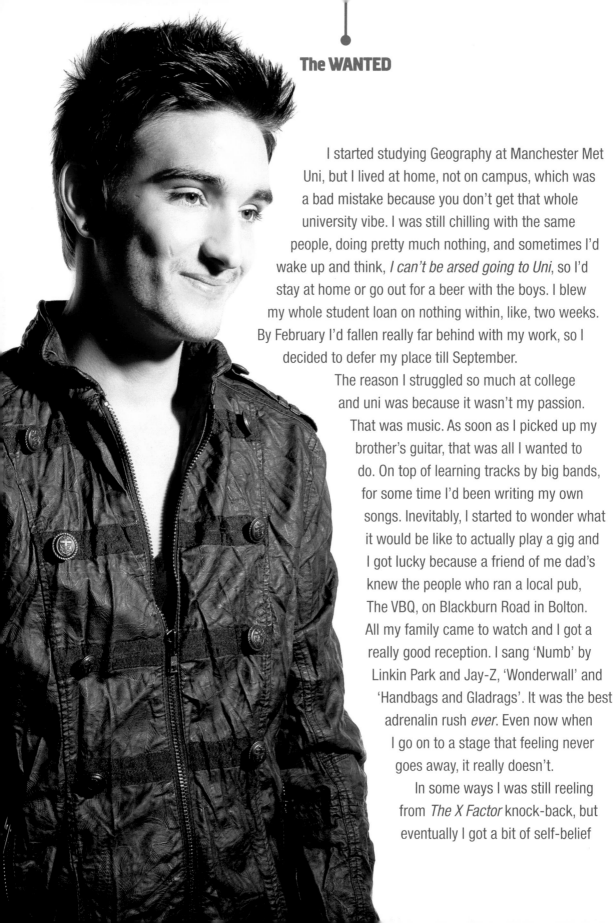

I started studying Geography at Manchester Met Uni, but I lived at home, not on campus, which was a bad mistake because you don't get that whole university vibe. I was still chilling with the same people, doing pretty much nothing, and sometimes I'd wake up and think, *I can't be arsed going to Uni*, so I'd stay at home or go out for a beer with the boys. I blew my whole student loan on nothing within, like, two weeks. By February I'd fallen really far behind with my work, so I decided to defer my place till September.

The reason I struggled so much at college and uni was because it wasn't my passion. That was music. As soon as I picked up my brother's guitar, that was all I wanted to do. On top of learning tracks by big bands, for some time I'd been writing my own songs. Inevitably, I started to wonder what it would be like to actually play a gig and I got lucky because a friend of me dad's knew the people who ran a local pub, The VBQ, on Blackburn Road in Bolton. All my family came to watch and I got a really good reception. I sang 'Numb' by Linkin Park and Jay-Z, 'Wonderwall' and 'Handbags and Gladrags'. It was the best adrenalin rush *ever*. Even now when I go on to a stage that feeling never goes away, it really doesn't.

In some ways I was still reeling from *The X Factor* knock-back, but eventually I got a bit of self-belief

even now when
I go on to a stage
that feeling never
goes away

back and started singing in pubs and clubs around
Bolton quite regularly. I started pushing myself more as
a singer, too, 'cos I knew I had to work hard to progress.
I went to live in Sheffield with my mate Ali for a year
and we did a little bit of writing together. I knew I had
a talent for writing as well as singing, and during those
months we helped bring each other on. All the time I was
performing regularly in the clubs and pubs in my area,
sometimes just vocals, sometimes live acoustic stuff,
and gaining loads of experience.

Then one day I was searching for auditions. I saw a
site for Jayne Collins Casting, so I applied to that and
went for an audition looking for talent to join Xenomania,
a huge UK music production team. That didn't work out,
but I did get a call-back from the same casting company
asking if I'd like to audition for a new band … and I
thought to myself, *Why not? Let's give it a go* …

The WANTED

AUDITIONS

Max: So I'd had this phone call from Ashley about a new band and travelled down to meet the music industry people who were involved. They were all big names in the business including Colin Barlow from Geffen Records (the man responsible for Take That's superb come back). Once I got there, it was explained to me what the project was and who the band would be working with. They were looking for five strong personalities, and the casting director, Jayne Collins, was one of the top names in the business, who we would later discover was to be our manager. When I saw the list of big-name songwriters and producers they were lining-up to work with the band, I was even more excited. I was offered a place in the band straight away, and I'll be honest, I didn't have to think twice before I said yes. It was difficult in the back of me mind 'cos I knew I'd be leaving the other lads in Avenue, but I'd done that band for nearly four years by then. Obviously I was chuffed about the offer, but I still wanted to audition: I didn't want to feel like I'd got in the band any differently to anyone else. There was going to be a series of auditions around about April 2009. I was taking a risk, though: they might have gone through the audition process and seen five other lads they thought were perfect instead and I was never guaranteed a place.

Nathan: At this point it was just me, Max and Tom auditioning. Jay and Siva didn't come along until much later. As I said, the Sylvia Young School sent every single boy in my year to the audition, so there were quite a few musical theatre kids there and at first I thought, *This could be really cheesy, perhaps I'd rather not get through?* But despite that, it was very interesting – for example it was my first

time singing in front of a flip camera. The people behind the auditions really seemed to want to find personalities as well as people who could sing, so later on we did some pieces to camera, like small interviews if you like.

Tom: At the time I did my first audition for this band, I was on Job-seeker's Allowance, just trying to find an opportunity. I didn't know then that the whole process would take over nine months. Obviously at that time I was pretty much in the dark about the music industry, I didn't know who was involved or anything, really. I just knew I had to go to auditions if I was going to get a break. My mate Ali kept taking me up and down from Sheffield to London for all the months it took, and my dad always gave me money to get there.

At the first audition I sang one of my own songs, 'Let It Go'. That might have been risky, but you gotta go into them places and be confident of your ability. I wrote the song when I was 16, six months after I first started playing guitar. They seemed to like it, though, because I got asked back.

The second audition was a disaster, though. I were playing guitar and felt really nervous. I just didn't perform well and thought I'd fluffed it, especially when I looked around at the competition sat in the corridor. I was like, *He's better than me.*

Halfway through the auditions, they told us we had a month to learn to dance before the next call-back. They told us about Pineapple Studios, but I was still living in Bolton with my mum, so my cousin Vicky, who's a trained dancer, gave me private lessons for free.

Max: I didn't realize they wanted people to dance, and I'd never danced before, ever! I was like, *What the hell is this?!* We had to do this big routine and I just couldn't do it. I got a bollocking after that audition because I didn't know what I was doing … I was gutted. They said to me on the phone afterwards, 'Your vocals are fine but you really need to improve on your dancing.' So I went away and my mate Jonny – who I'd been in Avenue with and who's a choreographer – taught me every day for a month. Then I went back and we had this new routine and I done it fine. I just didn't want to miss the opportunity, so when they'd said to me, 'You really need to improve your dancing,' I thought, *I might not get in here, I need to really get me head down.*

Tom: I was always intent on being at the front, just because I wanted to show everyone involved that I was trying my hardest. I wanna learn how to get better and I wanna prove to you that I've got the ability to do this.

Siva: The three other lads had done loads of auditions before me and Jay started. My first audition was in this church just off Tottenham Court Road. I was ridiculously nervous 'cos I hadn't sung in front of anyone for ages, I'd just been concentrating on modelling. I'd left my guitar in Ireland and hadn't had a chance to play it for months. I went in and sang 'Home', the Michael Bublé song, simply because I missed my family and friends back in Ireland so much.

I'd been having doubts about modelling for a while, and by the time this audition came up I'd set my hopes on a place at college – I'd been saving my money from modelling work so I could afford to study. I wanted to do a media course as I love

that industry. So when I went to The Wanted auditions, I was thinking, *Do your very best, but if you don't get it, just move on and go to college.*

Jay: I'll be honest, in some of the auditions I was awful and in some I was like, *Yeah, I've killed that, I can forget about worrying over that now!* I later found out that Max, Tom and Nath had been auditioning for ages, but me and Siva came in pretty late in the process. One of the early auditions was singing to camera in a church, there were lots of singing stints and stuff, but to be honest, I've had dance auditions that were a lot longer than that.

I was chuffed when they said we'd need to do some dancing next. I knew then I could forget about feeling nervous or awkward and not worry about looking like an idiot when I was singing. I could just dance.

Siva: The most demanding part of the audition process for me was the intensive four-day boot camp they held in the autumn of 2009. It was like an *X Factor* show, but without the crying! We were all put into different groups to test out the chemistry and see how we handled ourselves. The team holding the auditions were pretty strict.

Nathan: I sang my best and just kept on being called back and called back, and then eventually it was an audition in front of Jayne Collins. I was petrified of Jayne! I'd auditioned for her before and I knew she was at the top of the business and highly respected. I was absolutely petrified when I walked in and there she was. I was like, *Oh my God!*

By then I thought, *I'd quite like to get in this band, it's a good idea.* I sang 'Lately' by Stevie Wonder, but I thought I'd blown it because it was awful. I did loads of vocal ad-libs and felt it hadn't work. At least I got to finish the song, though; some of my mates only got to sing one line! I went out feeling devastated, and after two hours on the train home I was convinced I'd blown it – devoed. Then the next day I got a phone call, 'We wanna see you for our final audition …' I couldn't believe it.

The WANTED

For one of the final auditions we had to choose a song. Mine was 'Red' by Daniel Merriweather. I walked in, sat down at the piano and sang me heart out. I've been told that that was the audition that got me in. Someone even told me Jayne said it was one of the best auditions she'd ever seen, which I was chuffed to bits about.

Tom: For some reason – I can't remember why – I was walking through a forest with my friends when they phoned to say, 'We want you to come in for a meeting tomorrow at the record label's head office.' I got a Megabus Standard ticket as I couldn't afford to buy anything else – the best transport in the world! I caught the Megabus the next day and walked into the Geffen offices and into this meeting room, and there we were, all five of us.

Nathan: I walked in and was faced with Colin and Ashley, the music moguls of the project. The other four lads were already there, so we got a cup of tea together and went into the meeting room. We were like, 'What's this about then?!' We didn't have a clue. The others had got the same phone call as me, which hadn't told us why we were being called down to London. At one point, the record label bigwigs went to get a drink and Tom leaned over to me and said, 'Are you gonna ask or shall I?' So when they walked back in, Tom went, 'Er, is this the band or not?' And they said, 'Yes, it's you five. This is the band.' It had only been about five minutes but it felt like hours. *Right, now we can get excited!*

Jay: I didn't expect the band to be what it is. I thought it would be touring clubs and that I'd be lucky to get £200 a week, if that. So when the auditions started, I thought, *Well, I guess it's money for now*. But as time went on I realized that this was the real deal. When I heard about the people involved, I started to really want it. I thought, *They're trying to crack the charts here, not just make a bit of money for a couple of years. This is serious stuff*. I'd started off pretty casual, you know, thinking if I didn't get this then there'd be another 30 auditions that month to try, but by the end of the audition process I was *desperate* to get in the band.

these four other people know
exactly what I am going
through ... we are 'the five'

The WANTED

Tom: It was really exciting for all of us to be told we'd been chosen as the band. We all went home and started thinking about what would happen next. *But* – and it's a big but – then I got this phone call saying we had to audition again with another seven lads! I just kept thinking, *No way, there's a chance I might not get this after all. What's going on?* That was pretty tough.

Nathan: We all got that phone call and I was like, *What?!* I would have been devastated if I'd been kicked out at that stage.

Max: I was like, *What is going on here? I thought we were 'the five'?* But apparently we weren't, not yet anyway, so I just thought to myself, *Do the same again, Max, just concentrate and get on with the singing.* Although in one sense the other four lads were still strangers, we'd been in that meeting together when they'd told us we were 'the five', so in my head I already looked on them as my band mates. To suddenly think that could change – that either me, Tom, Siva, Jay or Nath could be out – was really weird.

Jay: That was hard, watching the seven 'new' lads re-audition for a band we all thought we were in. You were watching them thinking, *He's good, he dances well, he looks good*, doubting yourself, wondering if you were gonna make it after all.

Siva: They brought back seven other lads, including my brothers Trevor and Kumar, and they kept constantly switching between us. That was hard, obviously, but as brothers we just thought, *If one of us gets in … it would be brilliant for one of us to have that chance.* We all knew there was something special about this band.

Tom: They were constantly swapping Siva and his twin brother around, and I were like, *That is so unfair!*

Siva: That was a very long and nerve-racking day. Finally, after what seemed like for ever, our names were called out and there we were – the original five – standing looking at each other, thinking, *This is it … this is the band.*

there we
were thinking,
This is it ...
this is the band

The WANTED

Jay: At first I wondered why they were re-auditioning those seven lads again, but the fact that they chucked in every other combination and we were still the best line-up was wicked. They later told me they knew the five they wanted, they were just mixing things up with the seven other lads to make *absolutely* certain – double-checking really. 'Could it be better with this other guy perhaps?' And the answer was always, 'No, the original five is easily the best line-up.'

I only knew Siva well 'cos we were in the same harmony groups for the audition process – me, him and another lad. And before that I'd helped him, Kumar and Trev with some dancing stuff. Somehow, that last-minute audition where we all thought we might not get in really brought us together. It really strengthened us as a band, we became so loyal straight away.

Nathan: That final audition with the seven other lads thrown in definitely solidified us as a band. That was when I sensed the first bit of chemistry. Singing with this group of lads for the first time just felt right. There

were some great voices from the other lads they'd brought back at the last minute, but the harmonies of the original five just worked and you could tell that the people behind the auditions knew that vocally we were gelling as a band already. I didn't speak to all of the band all the time during the auditions, 'cos there were loads of people and you end up speaking to all sorts, but weirdly, even though we didn't know each other yet, it just felt right.

Jay: There's a massive element of luck involved: if my mum hadn't got injured, maybe I'd never have gone to tap and I'd still be sat at home eating crisps! The day after my first audition for The Wanted, I was busy again – I had that circus audition to go to.

Max: On that same day, when the record-company people kept us back, then sat us down and said we were definitely 'the five', I was so relieved. I'd had so much backing from my family since I was a kid and I didn't want to be a let-down for them. It was the end of a long audition and we couldn't wait to get started.

IN THE STUDIO

Jay: In that short period after we were told we'd made the band, we'd do stuff for a few days, then go back home. In between we'd all be Facebooking each other, saying, *What are we doing next week?* We were all so ready to go for it!

Nathan: I had plans to go to college in Gloucester and do my A levels and I did actually start the first year at Ribston High School. It was during that time I found out I was in the band, but it was really hard because I wasn't allowed to tell anyone.

We were all just talking on Facebook and then the girls at school were like, 'Who's this on your Facebook page?' I added Siva and loads of girls were like, 'Who is *that*?' Then Max was added and within ten minutes my phone had about fifty texts on it from girls asking about him. Nobody knew about the band at this point – when I'd gone to the auditions, I'd just told people I was ill. The head of my year knew, though. I sat her down and said, 'I need to tell you why I keep skiving off school, just so I don't get thrown out. I wouldn't tell you otherwise 'cos I'm not allowed. I'm in a band signed to Universal Records …' After that they kinda got used to me not being at school.

Tom: After we'd been chosen there was a two-week pause before it went crazy! While we'd been auditioning, plans and ideas were already being worked on, so it went mad pretty much straight away. We found out in January 2010 that we'd be flying to Copenhagen to record with the producer and songwriter Cutfather, then they told us the names of some of the other songwriters we'd be working with, such as Guy Chambers. I was blown away by the idea of working with people of that calibre. I remember thinking, *That's the guy who wrote* 'Angels', *stood right there in front of me.*

Max: Guy throws a mint party! It's been said to me that when we were in Copenhagen it was the first time we came together as a 'working band', and without a doubt that's true. We had such a good time there, and such a laugh. We got to know each other and we also recorded a couple of great songs, which really helped. Our second single, 'Heart Vacancy', was recorded over there, and when we'd finished it, we looked around at each other and thought, *We could be doing something really good here.*

it was the best moment of my life, and I'm sure I speak for the rest of the band when I say that

The WANTED

Nathan: I'd been in a studio many times before, while I was at Sylvia Young, so I kinda knew what was happening, but I was still only 16 when we flew out to Copenhagen. It was in the studio that I came up with the band name. People assume it's from the headline wording of the original audition advert, but it's not, that's completely coincidental. There's a track on the album called 'Let's Get Ugly' based on the Ennio Morricone theme for the classic Western, *The Good, The Bad and The Ugly*. We were using a sample of that and we just kept imagining a 'Wanted' poster with us lot on it – so that was that. It was in the studio that we started writing and working together. I think that's when we became an authentic, working band.

Siva: I'd been in a studio a couple of times back in Ireland, so I wasn't entirely unfamiliar with the surroundings, but that was years ago. Now we were in the same room as Guy Chambers, and people like Taio Cruz were working on songs for us; it was a whole other level.

Guy Chambers didn't even really 'meet' us; he just shook our hands and said, 'OK, go on and sing.' He wanted to hear us sing before we met properly. I was shaking in my boots. I sang, then came back in and couldn't even look at him. I was so embarrassed and self-conscious about my voice. He was really nice and said, 'I like the sound of your voice, we can definitely work with that. I think I can see a lot of good potential in your voice, a lot of huskiness. It's rich.' Then Max went in to sing and he has a belting, *amazing* voice and I thought, *Oh my God!*

We did a few songs in London and a few songs in Denmark, then we met Steve Mac, who's written songs for some of the biggest names in music. He was ridiculously good and had a real good control and knowledge of what he was doing.

Max: It was a shock to all of us walking into a studio and having Guy there. We thought, *What is going on?* I saw him, shook his hand and then one of the first things he said to us was, 'I've got a song here that I've written with Taio Cruz …' I was like, *What?!* I just kept thinking, *We're nothing; we are literally five lads that have gone through some auditions, and that's it.* That was the first song we did by Guy and Taio and it was called 'Made'.

Siva: OK, it's true. I do have silk sheets, I admit it. And I like to light incense candles to help me relax. I like to work hard and then totally chill out.

Max: I tell you what, though, I miss my dogs. I've got two. The biggest one is Elvis, he's a Dogue de Bordeaux and although he's only two years old he weighs eleven stone. He's a big softie, though, he just dribbles and loves to play. I can't have him in the house because we're travelling so much, so friends and family are looking after him while I can't. Pete, 17, is my best friend. He's a little warrior and he means the world to me.

Obviously we read the papers and stuff. Sometimes you see articles written 'linking' us with various famous women. They've linked Leona Lewis and Rihanna to various members of the band for example. It's weird 'cos I just look at it and think, *She must be gutted she's been linked wi' me!* Or, *Blimey, she's dropped her standards!* I feel for her, not for me.

Nathan: None of us are sane, we're all a bit weird. Just a bit out there. That's what keeps us so tight. We are all really good mates and that helps us enjoy it.

ON THE ROAD

Tom: At the same time as continuing recording tracks for the album and settling into life in the house, we started rehearsing heavily in preparation for going out on the road to do loads of gigs.

Siva: We were dying to work. We used to see other bands out there touring, but be careful what you wish for!

Max: We started our schools tour on 30 March 2010 at Addington High School in Croydon. I had a stinking head cold, but it was just brilliant. We were all a bit nervous, but as soon as we started singing the kids went mad, even though they didn't really know who we were. We just loved it. We were bouncing off each other having a great time, walking and dancing among the kids, high-fiving them all, and they were dancing and singing too. It was brilliant. There was plenty of gooning about, too, in the headmaster's office and on the tour bus.

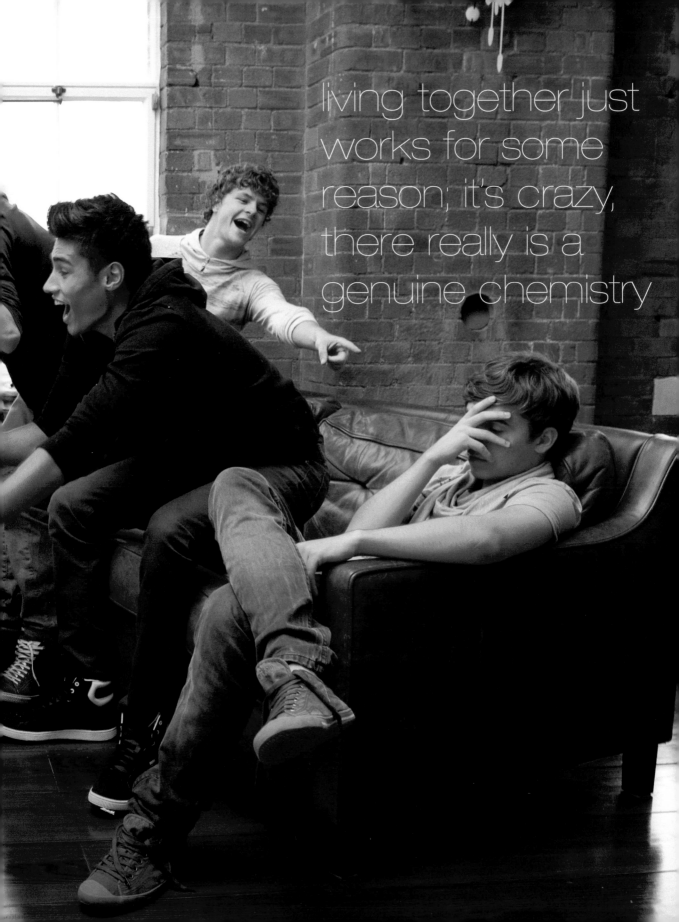

living together just works for some reason; it's crazy, there really is a genuine chemistry

Tom: It was brutal at times. Up at five, drive to a school show, back in the bus, over to another school, then sometimes an Under-18 club and maybe another club on the same night. We usually did three gigs a day, it was relentless.

Siva: Like Tom says, we were stuffed in the back of vans at five, six in the morning, we'd dash to a school then do a club gig at night, then the next morning up at six again for another early school show. It was gruelling but it really worked. The clubs just about paid for the school shows, but that wasn't the point. We didn't make any money, we made fans.

Jay: That schools' tour was when I first started seeing how excited people were getting about us. The thing about kids of that age is their reaction is *honest*. If they like you, they'll scream it out loud. But if they don't like you, they let you know just the same. Sometimes they'd stand there looking really bored and other times they'd openly boo you on stage. Fortunately, most of the kids were screaming their heads off.

Max: You might think it's a bit weird playing to 300 kids in the morning or the middle of the day with the lights on

full, but we didn't see it like that. We hadn't done anything yet as a band, so we didn't know any different and we loved it. Honestly, it was great. Those shows strengthened the chemistry we'd first felt in Copenhagen. We were really nervous at first, but once we were on stage we bounced off each other. We had such a good time and met so many lovely kids – and they're our fans now. Without them we wouldn't be anywhere.

Jay: We went to so many places. I was used to my dad working all over the country, but now the phone calls were coming from me in some far-away place. It gave me and my dad something to chat about, too. He'd say stuff like, 'Blackburn tonight, eh? I did the lights in the Co-op!'

Nathan: It was weird doing the school tour 'cos some places you'd go in and the reaction was as if we were The Beatles or something, but then at the next school you'd be treated like something they'd stepped on in the street. It was very hit and miss for a long time. At some schools, the girls would lie down in front of the van and refuse to move 'cos they didn't want us to go. Then at the next school they'd be like, 'Please go. We'll help you if you want. Here's your bags, get out.'

Girls throw stuff on stage. Usually it's bras, knickers and jewellery. Someone once threw a massive necklace at me and it cracked me right on the leg. I was singing and thinking, *Jeez, that really hurt!*

When I went back to my old school that was really weird! The last performance I'd done there was me sat at a piano, then I went back and took the boys from The Wanted in. The buzz about us on the internet had started by this time and the shows were getting more and more manic. The girls just went crazy. It was pretty strange seeing some of my sister's mates going absolutely wild. One of them even had 'Jay' written across her forehead.

Jay: When we played the older clubs I was pretty apprehensive to be honest. I've been to places like that and if a boy band had walked in they'd have been laughed off stage, but we just tried to enjoy whatever happened. Even if it was a rubbish gig we'd still have fun messing about. You have to laugh or you'd cry! In some clubs I'd be absolutely terrified, but Nathan was never bothered; he'd go out and get booed and still smile and perform his head off.

Max: We did one gig in a particularly rough club. The blokes were all standing there staring at us and there was a fair bit of jeering. The crowd just didn't like us! There were a few bottles thrown and all that, but I just thought it was funny; it was like being back in Manchester on a Friday night. People have asked us since if we were intimidated by gigs like that, and the honest answer is absolutely not, we just do what we do and we loved every minute of it – even those rough gigs.

Tom: Then – incredibly – in June we got a slot performing at the Capital Summertime Ball at Wembley Stadium! That was just surreal. We came up through a trap door

and out in front of 70,000 people; it was just, *Whoah!* When I were on stage I had a flashback to me just sat in the VBQ pub on the Blackburn Road playing my first ever gig. From that to this!

Nathan: The night before we'd been in Brighton singing in front of 70 kids, then the next day we sang at Wembley in front of 70,000. There's a YouTube clip of the day and pretty much all of us kept saying, 'We don't deserve this!' It was incredible.

Max: In the weeks before we went to Wembley, I was fine. I wasn't nervous at all. We did a soundcheck the day before and I was still just excited. I kept thinking, *This is gonna be amazing.* I couldn't wait. But then I woke up that morning and I was bricking it! I couldn't eat, I just couldn't get me head round what we were about to do. That continued literally until the second we came up through the stage, and as soon as I was up there it was like, *This is the best thing in the world! One of the best days of me life!* I know the rest of the lads felt the same … but there was no time to rest.

Tom: When it got to the end of June, we were looking and feeling physically exhausted. Getting sleep wherever we could, just two or three hours a night, which wasn't good. But you could see the band's momentum and profile building, and our fan-base was growing all the time. The hype in the music industry was telling us the band could be something really big.

Max: After we'd done a three-month stint without a day off, we finally had three days' rest. But rather than sit at home, we all flew out to Benidorm! I'm not sure the record label were too happy about it, but we needed to go, we were just like, 'We're off!' It was a proper lads' weekend. Great! Booze, sun and women. The perfect weekend for a lad.

Jay: At home after Benidorm it was straight back to the hard work again with a 4 a.m. start for *GMTV*. It was weird because we were working really hard but couldn't see any results yet. We were starting to get feedback, but if people asked me what I was doing, there was

nothing concrete to show them. People had no idea. I hadn't even told my family much about what I was doing for a while 'cos I'd had so much disappointment with auditions and work. I thought, *I'm not gonna excite everyone, then disappoint them all over again.*

Max: What we did know for a fact was that we had an amazing debut single in 'All Time Low'. What a song!

THE PATH TO NUMBER 1

Siva: When we first heard 'All Time Low' at the record-company offices, as soon as the strings kicked in all of our heads went down on the table and our eyes closed – we just *knew* that was the song for us. I got goosebumps all over.

Nathan: When the track was released on YouTube, a lot of people already knew about it. That's because our fans talk so much, there was a real-word-of-mouth feeling about it.

Max: Our fans have been amazing, they couldn't have supported us any better! We started doing a 'Wanted Wednesday' flip interview and Jayne videoed us pretty much everywhere. Fans sent in brilliant questions and we posted loads of other videos online too. It was great fun and felt like we were talking directly to our fans all the time.

Nathan: I was the only one that said we'd get Number 1. I'm quite a positive person and I said it in a car on the way back from a school show. 'I'm gonna say something now and you're not gonna like it … I think we're getting Number 1!' I got terrorized by the rest of the band. They couldn't believe I'd said it …

Jay: I just never considered anyone from the UK knowing anything about us. We'd spoken to so many people on Twitter and Facebook and had wicked feedback at gigs and schools, but there were people who'd slated us too. We had no idea

what league we were in. Then as the single release date approached, people were talking about the Top 50, then the Top 20, then maybe even the Top 10.

Max: In the week of the single's release, we did a load of signings and performances at record shops and shopping centres. They were rammed. We did loads of radio interviews, too, and there'd be all these fans waiting outside the station to say hello. We did wonder how well the single might do when we saw all those fans going mental, but you never know. When we got to Westfield shopping centre in London, we expected maybe a couple of hundred fans at the most, but there were something like 5,000 girls waiting to see us. We arrived at 4 p.m., performed on stage and signed our last autograph at 11 p.m.! It was a superb day!

Nathan: Westfield! What I can say? Wow! We sat down and did nearly six hours of signing. Everyone who was there wanted to see us. Some bands don't do pictures 'cos it takes ages, but we thought, *These fans have been waiting here for ages.* And it was good to just sit down and talk to them for a while.

Siva: On the morning of the single's release, we hit number 20 in the iTunes chart, then by around 9 o'clock that evening we were Number 1. That was very exciting and now we were anxious to see how the rest of the week panned out for the UK Top 40 Charts. As the week went by, the reaction at the signings told us we were doing well, but we were still thinking, *OK, exactly how did this happen?* It didn't seem real.

Also, Flo Rida's single was catching us, especially towards the end of the week; we were so nervous he'd overtake us!

Max: On the Sunday night when the charts were announced, the whole team got together and Colin and Ashley came over to have a chat with us and then, out of nowhere, they said, 'Guys, we'd like to thank you for all your work, and just tell you that you are at Number 1 in the UK charts.' At first we just sat there in silence, then we cried like babies. It was magic!

Tom: It was the best moment of my life, and I'm sure I speak for the rest of the band when I say that. Obviously I have a lot of happy memories growing up, but nothing can compare to that feeling of someone telling you that you are a UK Number 1 recording artist. I haven't cried like that for years. That achievement is set in stone. We are Number 1 forever, and it's something we can tell our kids and grandkids. It was like, 'We have done ourselves proud, boys!' All that hard work actually paid off. We were driven into the ground for three or four months, but it was so worth it and I wouldn't change it for the world. It looks like we came out of nowhere really fast but we'd put in a lot of groundwork before reaching Number 1.

Max: When we'd recorded 'All Time Low' in the studio, we knew it was a good song. That much was clear. We even thought, *This could actually be quite big*. But when we said 'quite big', we thought Top 100, not 'quite big' as in Number 1. We never expected that. What a moment!

THE FUTURE

Jay: Since the Number 1, we've not stopped for a second. It's been a blur of appearances, performances and visits to radio stations and studios. We travelled to Germany – where we even met The Hoff! – and there are plans for America … it's just insane.

Siva: Back when The Wanted first started, we'd have some work, then two weeks of waiting around; now we're lucky if we get a day off every two weeks. There is so much work involved, you need a real good work ethic. This isn't a 9 to 5 job. If you finish late one evening but then suddenly someone needs you to be somewhere else, you have to go. No ifs, no buts, just do it. You have to do it, because there are five of you. You need to keep that work ethic strong because if one of you isn't pulling their weight then it's going to break apart – everyone's plans are linked together. We are a *band*.

Tom: It's gone quite crazy to be honest. Everyone keeps comparing it to the Take That days, which is such a compliment, but I think we have a lot to prove before we're anywhere near that level. Hopefully we can be one day.

All of us in the band really appreciate the opportunity we've been given. Because we're all from working-class backgrounds, we don't take anything for granted. Sometimes we get free clothes and free food, free holidays even, and we're like, *What's going on here?!* We try to keep our feet on the ground.

Jay: We've met loads of celebrities now, and a lot of the time they come up to you like you should be bowing at their feet, and I feel really ignorant if I don't know who they are. I don't ever want to be that person who walks into a room and doesn't say their name 'cos they assume everyone knows who they are. What's that all about?

We know that we're in this bubble. We know everything we're doing every day and we see every article, we know every gig, but in reality you just don't know how far we've reached yet. The Number 1 was a massive indication that this thing has already got bigger than we thought. Who knows what's next?

Nathan: I feel like there's no limit to what we can achieve. We need to strive to keep on exceeding our own expectations, working really hard and just seeing where life takes us.

Max: We're having the most unbelievable time right now, and if it can continue for years then great; if not, then at least we can look back and say we literally had the time of our lives.

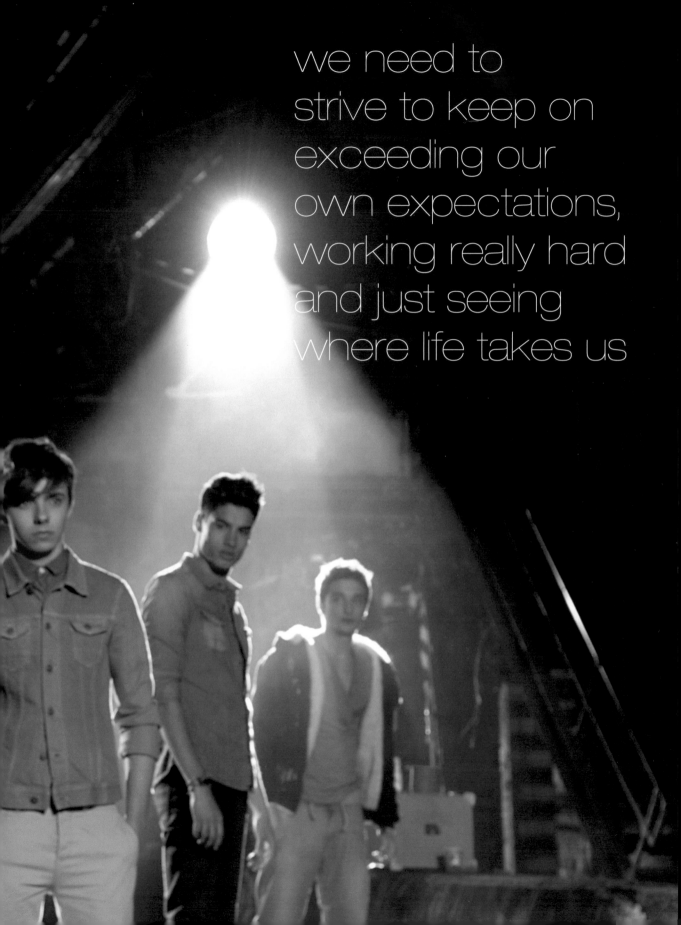

we need to
strive to keep on
exceeding our
own expectations,
working really hard
and just seeing
where life takes us

The WANTED

The WANTED

Jay: Our fans are just wicked. We spend so much time on Twitter and Facebook that we got really anti-social for a while. We really got into chatting with everybody. Now we know so many people that even when we're in front of a massive crowd, you look out and see maybe fifty people you've met at a club, or who've been emailing you for ages, and you give 'em a little wave. I never ever thought it would be like that, that you'd get to know fans this way.

Siva: Two situations stick in my head that sum up our fans. One time, me and Jay got out of a car at a radio station and there was a girl there wearing a shirt with 'Jiva' written on it, because she was a fan of both of us. That's incredible, so original, I loved it. What's more, she was there all on her own. Usually fans come along in a crowd, but this girl just wanted to say hello and support us; she didn't mind that she was on her own. Then, of course, there are the signings like the one at Westfield, which are insane. At lots of those events, we were disappointed for the fans when we noticed they had to cap the queues because it was getting ridiculous. We were gutted the first time it happened, but then at the very next signing, those same disappointed fans turned up to queue again – can you believe that? We are so lucky to have fans like that.

Nathan: It's really weird but great to know you can change someone's day just by sending them a tweet if they're having a bad time. You might say something like, 'I hope your day

gets better soon, babe,' and they'll tweet back saying it really put a smile on their face. That's really good to know. And it works both ways. If one of us gets bad press, the fans are always the first ones to support us. They let you know about the bad press as well! When I log on to Twitter someone might say, 'Nathan, I can't believe they said that about you!' And I'm like, 'Said what about me?!' They're just amazing.

Max: When you hear about all these things the fans have done, all the trouble they go to, all the effort they make, it's just amazing. I have christened our fans our 'Fan-mily'! Cheesey as, isn't it! But it's just because we appreciate them *so* much. How they've stood by us and followed us everywhere. Without them I don't know what I'd be doing. The word is *loyal*, that sums them up. They've been awesome, amazing.

Tom: The fans are a massive part of being in The Wanted, a huge part. The support they give us is incredible. We've always involved them in competitions and online videos and we will continue to try to interact with them as much as we can. I guess that makes the fans feel like they know us, and likewise we feel like we know them. We always remember their names – I was talking to a girl just the other day and she couldn't believe that I knew her name. But to us these are the people buying our records, coming to see our shows and making this possible, so it doesn't take much to remember their name or send them a little message. I just want our fans to know how much we appreciate them.

THE WANTED ♥

Mrs. Nathan Sykes

In your heart,
in your heart,
in your heart...
♥ 𝄞 ♫
Si-Si-Siva

GIV YOUTH

THANK YOU TO OUR FANS

Our fans mean so much to us that we wanted to find a way to get as many of you in the book as possible, to say thank you for all your support. Over the next few pages you'll find the lucky winners of our book competitions: Heart2Heart, Guest Interviewer and Quick Off the Mark. We were overwhelmed by the response we got. You guys are amazing! We'd love to put you all in the book, but unfortunately we've only got space for a few. Were you one of the lucky ones?!

HEART2HEART

On this and the previous page you'll find the lucky winners of our Heart2Heart competition (see also picture credits on page 192).

GUEST INTERVIEWER

We asked you to send in the most unusual questions you could think of that we haven't been asked before. Here is just a small selection of the best.

What inspires you to write a new song? (Kate Rodgers)
NATHAN: Being depressed in love.

Do you have any pre-show rituals or superstitions? (Rebecca Baker)
SIVA: Yes. I tie my right shoe lace very tight. Just something I always do.

What do you think about when you get nervous on stage (Sophie Lewsey)
JAY: I used to try and distract myself, but then I discovered that nerves are a good thing because they pump you full of adrenaline and make every performance exciting.

What do friends outside of the band think of your success? (Gemma Bayley)
JAY: Mostly they're gobsmacked as I'd be the last person to be picked for a boy band, but everyone is dead proud that someone from my area is involved and excited about seeing us grow.

Do you miss being able to go places without people recognizing you? (Evy Robinson)
SIVA: Not at all. Without fans we would not get anywhere and it's quite a compliment; it shows we are doing at least something right.

What has been your biggest challenge as a band? Have you been able to overcome that challenge? If so, how? (Emma Louise Balcers)
NATHAN: Being so shy off stage in the beginning, getting used to doing interviews and getting papped. I've learnt to accept these challenges and appreciate them as part of the job.

If you had to listen to one song for the rest of your life, what would it be?
(Sarah Marie Chambers)
JAY: 'Bohemian Rhapsody' because it's like seven songs in one!

The WANTED

What were your first impressions of each other when you first met? (Rachel Lawrie)
MAX: I though Nathan was a quiet boy, I looked out for him in the auditions, Jay was a real gentleman, Siva was his identical twin and Tom reminded me of being at Bolton market.

If you had to be one of the other Wanted members, who would you be and why? (Evie Miles)
JAY: I would be Nathan because I'd love to sit and play at the piano, but it would be weird to be short – the climate would be different down there!

When did you guys have your first kiss and where? (Victoria Lovelock)
TOM: My first kiss was in the cinema when I was 12 with a girl who bit my lip!

Who gives the best hugs? (Stephanie Crampton)
MAX: My dog Elvis.

What is your favourite childhood memory? (Jayne Entwistle and others)
NATHAN: Singing at Old Trafford (when I won that competition).

If you could be a girl for a day what would you do and why? (SophieC and others)
JAY: I would wink at all the boys just to give them a little gift of hope! And I would go to the Ladies' with the other girls and find out what they all gossip about!

What is the worst dare you have ever done? (Ellena Walker)
SIVA: I jumped off a high building into mud once, it was in someone's back garden. I wouldn't do that again.

Who is/are your idol(s)? (Lucy Cadman)
TOM: Liam Gallagher, John Lennon and The Beatles.

If you took over the world tomorrow, what would you want to do first? (Edwina Healey-Lapena)
NATHAN: Make it law that everyone has The Wanted album.

If you were granted the true answer to any one question in the universe, what would you ask? (Tammy Wooldridge)

TOM: Is there life after death?

If you could have one person from history as your assistant who would it be? (Daisy Andoh Cunnell)

MAX: The great Nelson Mandela.

Do you have any hidden talents? (Vanese Maddix)

SIVA: I can walk on my hands for 30 seconds, but then I always end up flat on my back.

What's Your Biggest Fear? (Kayleigh Papworth)

MAX: Failing.

One song to represent your life so far (Annabelle Kay)

JAY: I would pick 'Golden' which is a song on the album we wrote and it was about the process of struggling to get into the band and how it all turned out good. I think in life that is true; there is no use in worrying as it all turns out right in the end.

What motto do you live by? (Rachel Smith)

TOM: Live by the sword, die by the sword.

You've all come from different backgrounds to end up together, what advice would you give to someone who wanted to pursue a career in music (Nicole Kennedy and others)

NATHAN: Follow the dream, work hard, inspire and be inspired.

QUICK OFF THE MARK

We know the 'TWFanmily' are a dedicated bunch but we couldn't believe just how fast you were to respond to our competition! It took less than a minute for the winning entry to reach us after the post went up on Facebook, and all of the first fifty emails were received within two minutes. Wow! Here is the roll call of honour:

1. Sophie Louisa Cordell
2. Eve Smith
3. Lucy Archer
4. Faye Molly Fullerton
5. Alexandra Rowley
6. Rebecca Wilson
7. Alana Withersby
8. Clare Glynn
9. Jodee Lee Spencer
10. Lizzie Holman
11. Aneesa Siva Iqbal
12. Stacey Fenwick
13. Scott Davies
14. Amelia Birkin
15. Izzy Slocombe
16. Polly Freestone
17. Kezza Davenport
18. Lizzie Hancock
19. Tammy Wooldridge
20. Penny Crocker
21. Maisie O'Donnell & Georgia Gill
22. Harpeet Gill
23. Helen Roberts
24. Shannon O'Sullivan
25. Charlie Leavy
26. Nicola Craig
27. Jodie White
28. Katy Race
29. Eleanor Abbott
30. Chelsea Odonnell
31. Katie Rebecca Lewis
32. Justine Barnett
33. Annabelle Kay
34. Amina Sharif
35. Sam Watson (Samsam)
36. Olivia Smith
37. Ayisha Akamo
38. Sophy Blyth
39. Mahlet Tadesse
40. Lauren Ballantyne
41. Marika Moverley
42. Mollie Bolton
43. Beth Rose
44. Sophia Bray
45. Lizi
46. Chloe Verrier
47. Samantha Kate Bearman
48. Fiona Lawrence
49. Jenna, Penny, Shivonne & Leanne
50. Chloe Nicole Langton

BAND'S ACKNOWLEDGEMENTS

Thanks to 'Casper the friendly ghost writer' Martin Roach – an amazing writer & an amazing person (said in a whisper....).

To all the photographers involved in the making of this book.

Natasha Martin and all at Pan Macmillian.

To all our friends & family for all the love and support.... and funding!

Our amazing styling team Luke, Danielle, Eilidh, Luan, Debs & Dangerous Dave!

To Rob, Jayne and all our amazing team at Maximum Artist Management; music man & our guru Colin & everyone at Geffen and the legend that is Ashley & everyone at Global. You all believed in us right from the start (even though sometimes we can be a bit of a handful!)

To Sarah & David who spent many hours stressing about photographs and our dredful spellin and. punctuation,

And to the love of our lives .... Jayne, for all of the hard work she has put into bringing together what we feel is a great book and who I'm sure has wanted to kill us on many occasions throughout writing process!

And everyone who has brought us to the position where we can actually write a thank you in our OWN BOOK!!!!!

.... #itsaTWthing"